PURPLE HEART *and* THE INFIDEL

PURPLE HEART

and

THE INFIDEL

⊰TWO PLAYS⊱

BRUCE NORRIS

Foreword by John Guare

NORTHWESTERN UNIVERSITY PRESS

EVANSTON, ILLINOIS

Northwestern University Press
Evanston, Illinois 60208-4170

Printed in the United States of America

10 9 8 7 6 5 4 3 2 1

ISBN 0-8101-2214-6

LIBRARY OF CONGRESS
CATALOGING-IN-PUBLICATION DATA

Norris, Bruce.
    [Purple Heart]
    Purple Heart ; and The Infidel : two
plays / Bruce Norris ; foreword by John
Guare.
        p. cm.
    ISBN 0-8101-2214-6 (trade paper :
alk. paper)
    1. Psychology—Drama. I. Title:
Purple Heart ; and, The Infidel.
II. Norris, Bruce. Infidel. III. Title:
Infidel. IV. Title.
PS3614.O768P87 2004
812'.54—dc22
                              2004023283

⊗ The paper used in this publication meets
the minimum requirements of the American National Standard for Information Sci-
ences—Permanence of Paper for Printed
Library Materials, ANSI Z39.48-1992.

With many thanks to Anna Shapiro, Michelle Volansky,
Ed Sobel, Laura Glenn, Mary Harden, Nancy Curtis,
casts, designers, crews, but especially to Martha Lavey
and Steppenwolf Theatre Company, whose continued
support I hope, eventually, to deserve.

CONTENTS

FOREWORD
John Guare

Bruce Norris is an actor I admire tremendously; he's quirky, wildly intelligent, extraordinarily funny. When he and the part he's playing connect, he is a playwright's dream. We became friends in 1998 after he appeared in a play of mine at the Signature Theatre in New York. He played the part just as I had imagined it. I then wrote a play for him called *Chaucer in Rome,* which we did at Lincoln Center. I keep his performance in that play up there in my memory bank along with Swoosie Kurtz in *The House of Blue Leaves,* Stockard Channing in *Six Degrees of Separation,* Polly Holliday, John Mahoney, Raul Julia—those perfect performances that make you glad you're a playwright.

But when Bruce Norris gave me a play to read called *The Infidel,* I have to confess I groaned. I know what happens when an actor writes a play. It contains a big fat juicy part for him or her and nothing for anybody else. OK, Molière, Noël Coward, and Mae West come to mind—which is fine if you're Molière or Noël Coward or Mae West.

Bruce Norris's play surprised me first of all because there was no role in it for him. I recognized the story, which had made a big splash in the news a few years before—an important judge ruins his life by stalking a woman with whom he is obsessed. What surprised me about *The Infidel* is that it's not a variation of *The Blue Angel,* wherein the power of lust brings down and humiliates the man of dignity. Bruce Norris presents a man who is (and this is the surprise and the reward) dignified by his emotion. Also, the play was deeply felt, deeply lived. This was not the Bruce Norris I knew. His play reminded me somewhat of Pinter, not in its manner or verbal rhythms but in the way Bruce Norris puts his magnifying glass over a world recognizable on the surface and we find we've tumbled into a world where the nightmare is love—who it is we powerlessly fall in love with. What's so original about *The Infidel,* and his subsequent plays such as *Purple*

Heart, is that he writes of people unable to control their lives because the affliction of love has taken control and drives them to places they did not know existed.

The plays in this volume made me realize I didn't know Bruce Norris at all. I knew that he was an unlikely Texan from Houston born in 1960, that he had been a child actor at the Alley Theatre, that his father was some kind of successful doctor, and that he had gone to Boston University as a scenic designer but transferred after a year to Northwestern as a theater major. He moved in with a classmate, the director Mary Zimmerman, who would years later win a Tony for her direction of *Metamorphoses,* and they shared an intense relationship that lasted sixteen years. He appeared in many plays in Chicago and New York and even starred in a very short lived TV sitcom called *The Popcorn Kid.* When he was cast in that, Bruce said he saw the beginning of the end: that he'd soon end up as a side square on *Hollywood Squares.* He fled back to Chicago and New York, where he was a highly regarded young actor, particularly effective in plays like Joe Orton's *What the Butler Saw* at the Manhattan Theatre Club.

And now he'd written a play. I knew he'd successfully adapted a Joe Orton screenplay, *Up Against It,* for Lookingglass Theatre in Chicago in the early nineties as well as the book and some of the music and lyrics for the very peculiar rock musical *The Vanishing Twin,* which he described as *Jane Eyre* in drag: "It had a very loyal following of about six high school girls." But these plays were the stuff of funny anecdotes. I was not prepared for *The Infidel* nor the play that came after, *Purple Heart.* From what mysterious well did Norris haul up these deeply felt plays? I sat down with Bruce Norris to have the kind of talk we had never had. This is what he told me. (You have to realize that he speaks in passionate, fully formed paragraphs.)

BN: The inspiration for *The Infidel* had to do with a personal crisis in my life when I was in my midthirties and found myself in a humiliatingly obsessive sexual situation that I had to conceal for various reasons. I found myself following this woman, spying on her. In the middle of this crack-up, I was doing a production of *Three Sisters* at the Goodman, playing Baron von Tusenbach. I didn't ever feel I was this big emotional actor, but I'd get to the fourth act, where Tusenbach goes off to duel, and I found myself dripping tears every night because of where I was at this point. My mother had died. I wanted to talk to my father, even though I knew I wouldn't get any response or help from him. Still I made the decision to tell my father the whole ugly story of this emotional, embarrassing, sexual situation I had got caught up in. I told him all the details of it. He had absolutely nothing to say, and yet I felt much better having said what I said. I had spent so much of my life concealing anything intimate or personal from my father. But this time I insisted he hear me. Afterward I felt as if I'd broken through some obstacle with him and that he wasn't afraid of me anymore. Or me of him. And I moved to New York.

JG: And then one day you just started to write *The Infidel*.

BN: No, Steppenwolf Theatre had commissioned me to write a play, which I've now hidden away for good, called *Blue Bonnet State*, which is autobiographical in a not very successful way that you have to get out of your system. They did a reading of it. I was in it, but that was part of the problem with it. It had that kind of self-aware autobiographical voice to it. And I didn't like that voice. Martha Lavey of Steppenwolf said, Why don't you take another shot, and they commissioned me for a second year.

JG: And that turned out to be *The Infidel*.

BN: Yes.

JG: Why did Steppenwolf commission you?

BN: It's total Chicago old boy network, or old girl network. Martha Lavey acted in the very first play I wrote and got produced in Chicago in '91 or '92. It was called *The Actor Retires* and literally was a vanity project because it was about my own inability to deal with vanity, the actor's narcissism, the actor's twin hats of being grandiose and groveling. People thought I was writing about how stupid L.A. is, but that wasn't it at all. Its characters, the producers, directors, whoever was being parodied, are portrayed as normal people, whereas the sick one is myself. It was also a vanity project because I was in it. Had I let someone else be in it, perhaps I wouldn't think of it that way. But thanks to Martha Lavey, I got a second chance. I thought of that story of the New York judge who stalked the woman, with which I identified to an alarming degree, although I didn't go to prison.

Steppenwolf produced *The Infidel*, directed by Anna Shapiro, to a very positive response. And it was very scary because I was writing for voices that weren't familiar to me. Because *The Infidel* had no part for me in it, I felt it was my first real play. It was as if Steppenwolf was saying to me, We're going to produce this play with you not as a performer, not as a scene designer, not as a director, but as its writer. That they had faith in the play based solely on its merits, that was graduation.

JG: Steppenwolf then commissioned another play.

BN: Yes. *Purple Heart* was a different kind of autobiographical play. I didn't have to stick to the facts. The father in that play is a military man. My father was a doctor, internal medicine, arthritis his specialty. He was a disciplinarian who ran the house with enormous pressure to behave in a compliant fashion. And that had to do with attitude, with language. I got in very big trouble once because I used the word "hooker" and he asked me where I had heard that word. I claimed innocence by saying I'd heard it on the radio and didn't know what it meant. He kept a very strict, orderly household. My mother was the complete opposite, a very entertaining person to be around, very lively and fun and subversive. She had once entertained aspirations of being a painter or a costume designer but gave those up to raise my brother and sister and me and play the role of good wife and mom to my father and us. Her life somehow became unbearable and she turned into a serious drinker. I had every opportunity as a kid to see that she was in trouble, but I was so busy acting in local productions of things like *The Sound of Music* that I found it easy to look the other way—a fact that still bothers me. I, just like in *Purple Heart,* had a grandmother who would visit us from time to time and take me aside to explain that Mother had a drinking problem, which was why she was always asleep or going away for long periods of time. That's how it appears in the play. Both of these plays are about something deeply personal to me, but I don't consider either of them to be directly autobiographical. They're both about things that frightened me in my life, and they're both about things that have to do with love. In *The Infidel,* a powerful man has a tortured relationship between his sexual feelings and his romantic feelings. In the case of *Purple Heart,* it's a man who has a thwarted love relationship with a woman. Both plays share a vexed relationship between a man's sexual feelings and his romantic feelings for a woman, and those irreconcilable feelings are something I was going through at this time.

JG: It gave Strindberg enough to write on.

BN: I love Strindberg.

JG: What other plays do you like?

BN: I'm a big fan of Joe Orton. I love comedies from the middle of the twentieth century, Kaufman and Hart, Hecht and MacArthur, *The Front Page.*

JG: The playwright Bruce Norris becomes very quiet when he leaves New York, but didn't you have yet a third commission from Steppenwolf?

BN: We did the third play last year, *We All Went Down to Amsterdam.*

JG: That's the one that won a Jefferson Award for best new work.

BN: Yes. That's the one I feel no one has read or seen and it's almost the one I'm sort of proudest of.

JG: And not that I'm jealous or anything like that, but what are you doing next?

BN: Steppenwolf has commissioned *The Pain and the Itch*, which is a dark, tragic farce, but it moves back and forth across time.

JG: So, the other playwright says without any envy at all, soon you'll have had four plays done at Steppenwolf. How nice for you. How many other writers have had that kind of connection with that theater?

BN: I was told only one. Sam Shepard has had like six productions, but I'm next.

JG: Like Sam Shepard, do you think of yourself more as a playwright-actor, an actor-playwright, a playwright who acts?

BN: I guess I think of myself as a professional actor who works as an amateur playwright because I don't really make my living from being a playwright and I kind of prefer it that way. It's like being a professional poet. I don't think there are that many. I prefer to keep making my living as an actor because I feel like writing is too hard.

JG: The Bruce Norris who writes and the Bruce Norris who acts—are they two different human beings?

BN: Completely. One is a social activity, the other is very private. The playwright has to become social to collaborate, but acting involves responding, whereas writing is—I don't want to talk about it.

JG: You get up every day and write?

BN: In the afternoon. I usually have to leave my apartment early to do actor things.

JG: Can you write when you're in a play?

BN: Actually, that's helpful, especially when I'm performing at night. That's always a good way to organize the day. I wake up late and then I write. It's harder if you're working on a film because the times you're called change every day. That's why I'm trying to get a job in a play right now. I'd love to get a new play written.

JG: Do you dream differently as a writer than as an actor?

BN: Let me see. I dreamt last night that my hair was all burned off except for a ring of hair around the edge of my scalp. I looked in the mirror and there was an enormous scar slicing across my scalp. Does that count?

JG: I'd say it does. That dream has it all: flames, mirrors, vanity, wounds within the head. No doubt about it. Bruce Norris is a writer. What's the role you'd most like to play?

BN: The Misanthrope.

JG: Why?

BN: It's the only role I feel I truly identify with.

Read these plays by Bruce Norris. Welcome a valuable, striking, passionate, original, surprising new voice into the American theater.

PLAYWRIGHT'S NOTE

Both of these plays seem long on the page but move quickly when read aloud. The director of both original productions and I found that it was useful, in many instances, to encourage the actors to disrespect the sanctity of their fellow actors' lines and cues. This is truer for *Purple Heart* than for *The Infidel,* but in both we found numerous places where the spoken lines, by their nature and construction, benefit from a kind of engineered cacophony that may feel confusing and frustrating at first but ultimately sounds closer to what I intended. Obviously, this is not universally true, but I would particularly suggest it in Garvey and Helen's exchanges in *The Infidel* and those between Grace and Carla in *Purple Heart.*

PURPLE HEART

PRODUCTION HISTORY

Purple Heart was first produced by Steppenwolf Theatre Company (artistic director, Martha Lavey) on July 5, 2002. It was directed by Anna D. Shapiro, with set design by Daniel P. Ostling, costume design by James Schuette, lighting design by James F. Ingalls, and sound design by Rob Milburn and Michael Bodeen. Laura D. Glenn was the stage manager.

Thor . . . . Nathan Kiley
Carla . . . . Laurie Metcalf
Grace . . . . Rosemary Prinz
Purdy . . . . Christopher Evan Welch

The production then appeared at the Galway Arts Festival, Town Hall Theatre, Galway, Ireland, on July 23, 2003.

Thor . . . . Lucas Ellman
Carla . . . . Laurie Metcalf
Grace . . . . Rosemary Prinz
Purdy . . . . Matt Roth

CHARACTERS

Thor, twelve, wears long hair and tinted aviator glasses

Carla, thirties

Grace, sixty-five, wears a hearing aid

Purdy, twenties, large and polite, wears short hair,
glasses, and a corporal's uniform

STAGING

The set is the living room of Carla and Thor's home in a medium-sized city in the Midwest. The house has exits to a kitchen and dining room, one to the front door, and another to a hallway off of which other rooms are located. We can see down the hallway, but the front door is not visible. The house was built in the late fifties but has been decorated tastefully in the modern way, with shag rugs, contemporary lighting fixtures, and so forth.

There is no music in the play except where indicated.

The time is late October 1972.

ACT ONE

[*Six* P.M., *central daylight time. The room is almost totally dark.* THOR *enters from the hallway. He turns on a lamp, illuminating* CARLA, *who is asleep on the sofa. She wears a bathrobe over her clothes.* THOR *studies her briefly, then makes a circuit around the room, turning on other lights.* CARLA *remains asleep.* THOR *goes to the stereo and picks up a record. He places it on the turntable, then leaves the room. An aggressive rock song begins to play loudly.* CARLA *remains asleep.* THOR *re-enters with a stepladder. He places it near a wall and climbs up. He removes a clock from the wall and opens its back.* GRACE *enters from the front door. She wears a coat and scarf and carries her purse.*]

GRACE: Thor?

[THOR *does not respond. She patiently repeats herself.*]

   Thor? Thor? Thor? Thor?

[*She takes the needle off the record.*]

Thor.

[THOR *still does not respond.*]

I'm speaking to you, Thor.

THOR: I know.

GRACE: I'd like you to answer me when I speak to you.

THOR: I'm answering.

GRACE [*referring to the clock*]: What are you doing with that?

THOR: Changing the time.

GRACE: Did you ask before doing that?

THOR: No.

GRACE: Is there something wrong with it?

THOR: No.

GRACE: Maybe we should leave it the way it is.

THOR: Spring forward, fall back.

GRACE: Oh, I see.

THOR: I'm doing them all.

GRACE: I see now. Well. Thank you, then. And you know what you're doing?

THOR: It is oh so challenging.

GRACE: It *is* an expensive clock, Thor.

THOR [*innocently*]: Did you pay for it?

GRACE: I think we ought to ask your mother before we do something like that.

THOR [*to* CARLA]: Mom, can I set the clock back?

[CARLA *does not stir.*]

She doesn't mind.

GRACE: I don't trust that ladder. Is that ladder safe?

THOR: I don't know.

GRACE: Let's avoid having an accident.

[GRACE *exits down the hallway.* THOR *puts the clock back on the wall and climbs off the ladder. He sits next to* CARLA.]

THOR: She's back.

[CARLA *does not stir.* THOR *continues patiently.*]

Mom. Mom. Mom. Mom.

[*He takes her arm and removes her wristwatch. He resets the time, then returns it to her wrist.*]

Mom. Mom. Mom.

[*He pinches her nose. She pulls her head away but does not open her eyes.*]

CARLA: Don't.

THOR: She's back.

CARLA: Don't do that to me.

THOR: You said wake you up when she got back.

CARLA: I'm awake.

THOR: Now you are.

CARLA: Don't pinch my nose.

THOR: Get up.

CARLA: I'm up.

THOR: No, you're not.

CARLA: Go away.

THOR: Lazy ass.

CARLA: Go away.

THOR: Lazy ass.

CARLA: Watch it.

THOR: Lazy fucking ass.

CARLA: You're about to get your ass *whipped*.

THOR: I'm scared.

CARLA: Keep it up.

THOR: Like to see you try.

CARLA: Keep it up.

THOR: You'd have to get off your ass first.

CARLA: Keep it up.

THOR: Your lazy ass.

CARLA: Toilet mouth.

THOR: Ass face.

CARLA: I'm not going to speak to you.

THOR: What a tragedy.

CARLA: I'm not going to speak to a toilet mouth.

THOR: Oh, no. Not speak. Please. Anything but that.

[*Long pause.*]

Ahhh. Peace and quiet. Peace at last.

[*He grows restless.*]

Did I get my package?

[CARLA *does nothing.* THOR *kicks her.*]

Answer me. Where is it? Answer me. Cut it out. Answer me.

[CARLA *sticks out her tongue.*]

God, you're ugly. Old and lazy and ugly. Answer me. Did it come?
Stop it.

[CARLA *wiggles her tongue.*]

God, you're disgusting. You look disgusting when you do that.
Stop it. Answer me. I hate you. Lazy whore.

[CARLA *opens her eyes and sits up.*]

CARLA: *Hey.*

THOR: *What?*

CARLA: *Watch what you say to me, you little piece of shit.*

THOR: *So try answering me for a change.*

CARLA: *I did answer you, but you better watch your mouth.*

THOR: *No you didn't.*

CARLA: *Don't do things to me while I'm asleep.*

THOR: *You said to wake you up.*

[*Pause.*]

CARLA: How long has she been back?

THOR: Couple of minutes. Where is it?

CARLA: Where is what?

THOR: My package. I asked you ten times.

CARLA: I don't know.

THOR: Why is it taking so long?

CARLA: I don't know.

THOR: Fucking rip-off.

CARLA: It'll come.

THOR: When?

CARLA: I don't know.

THOR: Never.

CARLA: Maybe tomorrow.

THOR: Maybe never.

CARLA: Few more days.

THOR: I better get some money back.

[THOR *reaches into his pocket and pulls out a novelty finger guillotine.*]

Put your finger in here.

CARLA: No.

THOR: Do it.

CARLA: I don't want to.

THOR: Do it.

CARLA: No.

THOR: Do it.

CARLA: No.

THOR: *Yes.*

CARLA: I don't want to.

THOR: You have to.

CARLA: I'm not going to do it.

[THOR *finds a pencil, inserts it in the guillotine, and chops it in half. Then he pulls a trick knife and a tube of fake blood from his pocket and holds the knife to his throat.*]

THOR: Look.

CARLA: No.

THOR: I'm gonna stab myself.

CARLA: No.

THOR: Look. You *baby.*

CARLA: All right, all right.

[*He pushes the knife into his throat while squeezing the fake blood on his neck.*]

Very funny.

THOR: I'm bleeding.

CARLA: Don't get that on the sofa.

THOR: I'm dying.

CARLA: I don't want that blood on the sofa.

THOR: It washes out.

CARLA: I don't want to wash it out.

[*He wipes the blood off his neck.*]

THOR: What happened to Chet and Gibby?

CARLA: How should I know?

THOR: They never come over.

CARLA: They have their own things to do.

THOR: Like what?

CARLA: I don't know and frankly I don't care.

THOR: Call them.

CARLA: They go to college, Thor.

THOR: So?

CARLA: So the whole world doesn't revolve around you.

THOR: Yes it does.

CARLA: Fine. They're your friends.

THOR: They like *you.*

CARLA: You call them.

THOR: Where do I get the number?

CARLA: I don't know.

[*Pause.* THOR *takes something out of his pocket.*]

THOR: Oh no. I feel sick.

CARLA: Don't do that.

THOR: I'm gonna be sick. I'm gonna puke.

CARLA: I've seen it.

THOR: Oh no. Here it comes. Look. Look. Watch. You're not looking.

CARLA: All right. I'm looking.

THOR: Oh no. Oh no.

[*He makes a gagging noise and drops plastic vomit on the coffee table.*]

Ahhh. That's better.

CARLA: Very good.

THOR: Looks real.

CARLA: Very real.

[GRACE *enters, carrying a laundry basket. At the sound of her voice,* THOR *picks up the vomit and starts out of the room.*]

GRACE: Yoo-hoo? Here I am. So, are you awake then, dear?

CARLA: Yes. Hello.

GRACE: Thor?

THOR [*stopping*]: What?

GRACE: Where are you going?

THOR: My room.

GRACE: Have you been inside all day?

THOR: Mostly.

GRACE: Maybe you'd like to go *outside* on the weekends.

THOR: What for?

GRACE: Some fresh air.

THOR: My window is open.

GRACE: Or a little exercise. Where's your football?

THOR: There's no air in it.

GRACE: Why don't you see if you can find the pump?

THOR: Then what?

GRACE: Tomorrow you could play with it.

THOR: By myself?

GRACE: With one of your friends.

[THOR *stares at her for a moment, then walks out of the room.*]

[*To* THOR *as he leaves*] I hope you're going to put this ladder away. [*To* CARLA] That ladder is a crisis in the making.

[CARLA *does not respond.*]

I don't suppose you had a chance to go to the market.

CARLA: I wasn't feeling very well.

GRACE: Yes.

CARLA: Sorry.

GRACE: But you're feeling better now.

CARLA: A little better.

GRACE: You needed the rest. It's your stomach again?

CARLA: Mm-hmm.

GRACE: Did you find the milk of magnesia?

CARLA: No.

GRACE: Did you look next to my bed?

CARLA: Not really.

GRACE: Why don't I get it for you?

CARLA: I'm better now.

GRACE: I'm happy to do it.

CARLA: I'm fine.

GRACE: All right, then. I'm glad you're feeling better.

CARLA: Thanks.

[*Pause.*]

GRACE: Unfortunately, we are still out of milk.

CARLA: Oh. You didn't stop, then?

GRACE: Well, you had suggested that *you* would.

CARLA: I can still go.

GRACE: If I had known that you weren't going I would have been happy to go. But I was under the impression that you had gone. The pastor drove me right past the market.

CARLA: Okay.

GRACE: Right past without even slowing down. And there's very little butter.

CARLA: I'll put on some clothes and go.

GRACE: The butter isn't important. I can cook with the Crisco oil.

CARLA: Just give me a couple of minutes.

GRACE: But I do prefer milk for my coffee. [*Laughs.*] If it's between that and Crisco oil.

CARLA: No, I know.

GRACE: And I suppose we don't really need a green salad.

CARLA: There's lettuce.

GRACE: Yes.

CARLA: Look in the crisper.

GRACE: I did.

CARLA: There's a whole head of lettuce in there.

GRACE: Well, it seems to have rather wilted.

[*Pause.*]

CARLA: Give me three minutes and I'll go.

GRACE: Well, the market's closed, dear.

CARLA [*looking at her watch*]: They close at six.

GRACE: It's six-thirty.

CARLA: It's *five*-thirty.

GRACE: No.

CARLA: Look at the clock.

GRACE: No, Thor changed the clock.

CARLA: Why?

GRACE: And I suppose he must have changed your wristwatch as well.

CARLA: *It's five-thirty.*

GRACE: Tomorrow at this time it will be five-thirty, *standard* time. Right now it is actually six-thirty *daylight* time.

CARLA: Oh.

GRACE: He did us a little favor before we go to sleep.

CARLA: Oh.

GRACE: So I think we'd best abandon our plans concerning the market.

CARLA: Well. In that case.

GRACE: Doesn't matter to me. I'm happy to have a ham sandwich. There's still a good amount of that ham left. I love a nice ham sandwich and a glass of . . . [*Realizing*] Well, I don't suppose it has to be a glass of milk.

CARLA: I'll go first thing tomorrow.

GRACE: Would you care for a ham sandwich?

CARLA: I'm not hungry.

GRACE: Well, I believe I will. That ham that Mrs. Lacy brought over is *very* tasty, I have to say. Certainly no more difficult to make two. But I won't press. Thor, however, would probably prefer some sort of hot dish. We had the noodle casserole from the Osterbergs, but I believe that's gone bad.

CARLA: I'm sorry I didn't go, Grace. I had every intention of going. I'm sorry.

GRACE: No apology necessary. Oh, yes. Let's see. The pastor wanted to know if tomorrow at two would be a good time.

CARLA: Tomorrow?

GRACE: Or did you have plans?

CARLA: Not exactly.

GRACE: What are your plans?

CARLA: I don't have plans.

GRACE: Don't change them if you have them.

CARLA: I don't have them.

GRACE: So two is all right, then.

CARLA: What does he want to talk about?

GRACE: He's interested in how you are doing.

CARLA: But I spoke to him on the phone.

GRACE: Briefly.

CARLA: I told him I was doing fine.

GRACE: Wouldn't a visit be that much more pleasant?

CARLA: What time tomorrow?

GRACE: Two. After the second service.

CARLA: I . . . I . . . I don't . . .

GRACE: That way you'll be able to speak freely.

CARLA: Did he say I wasn't speaking freely on the phone?

GRACE: No.

CARLA: What am I supposed to speak freely *about*?

GRACE: I don't know.

CARLA: Freely. How freely does he want me to speak?

GRACE: I don't know.

CARLA: I'll be happy to speak freely. In fact, don't just bring the pastor. There has to be one or two people in the neighborhood who haven't stopped by. Bring 'em along. We'll do it in shifts. Bring the congregation.

GRACE: It is traditional. For the clergy to participate.

CARLA: In my life?

GRACE: In the grieving process.

CARLA: Let me see how I feel.

GRACE: Well, he is *planning* to come at two.

CARLA: So asking me was just a *formality*.

GRACE: I'll call him now if you'd rather reschedule.

CARLA: No.

GRACE: But that is his plan.

[*Silence for a few moments.*]

CARLA: Two is fine.

GRACE: I'll see what we have to make a hot dish.

CARLA: *What* time is it?

GRACE: It's six-thirty.

CARLA: That clock is crooked.

[*No one moves.*]

GRACE: Did the doctor say anything?

CARLA: Well. You know. I'm run down. The hospital didn't catch the anemia, so that's worse. And on top of that the upset stomach. Probably some kind of virus, he said, some kind of, I don't know, some kind of twenty-four-hour kind of thing. That sort of thing. You know. That kind of thing. He wasn't very specific.

GRACE: He didn't say anything else?

CARLA: Like what?

GRACE: I don't know.

CARLA: What kind of thing do you mean?

GRACE: That's what I'm asking *you*.

CARLA: What else would he say?

GRACE: Something more specific.

CARLA: I just told you what he said.

GRACE: All right.

CARLA: I don't understand what you're asking.

GRACE: He didn't give you anything?

CARLA: What would he give me?

GRACE: He didn't *prescribe* anything.

CARLA: No.

GRACE: All right. I will offer the milk of magnesia once again.

CARLA: No thanks.

GRACE: Well. The offer stands.

[*Pause.*]

CARLA: I was just *resting*, Grace. I just needed to *rest*.

GRACE: I know.

CARLA: It's not . . . I mean, it's not . . . I haven't been *feeling* well and . . .

GRACE [*overlapping*]: I understand that.

CARLA: . . . if I happen to need to *rest* from time to time I don't see anything particularly *sinister* in that . . .

GRACE [*overlapping*]: I don't say that there is.

CARLA: . . . I just need to *rest* and even though I know you *say* that, still there are these . . . these . . . these . . . these *silences* and you know being sick is not . . . especially given the . . . *circumstances* . . .

GRACE [*overlapping*]: I fully understand.

CARLA: . . . what I'm saying is being sick is not a *crime*, it's not an indication of some terrible *failure* or . . . or . . . I mean Jesus Christ people get sick and I'm terribly sorry that I happen to be one of those people. You've never gotten sick a day in your life of course you would never do that but God forbid you ever *do* I mean God forbid because what would that say about *you?* I'd hate to think.

[*Pause.*]

GRACE: No need to swear, dear.

CARLA: Sorry.

GRACE: So many other ways to express oneself.

CARLA: Right.

GRACE: Your mind is too original for that.

[*Pause.*]

Well, let's see. My day was rather interesting. Esther and I had lunch at the Pantry with Esther's friend Joanne Nierengarten. It turns out that Joanne's husband had esophageal cancer. Seems they had to remove a substantial amount of his esophagus and refashion the rest out of the existing stomach tissue, which to me just sounds like a hideous procedure. There's one thing to be grateful for. We have our health. Never overlook the blessing of good health. Did you know that the Pantry has taken the Neptune salad off of the lunch menu? I told the girl I had ordered that salad for the last twenty-five years and it simply baffled me that they would make such an arbitrary decision. She said we can make it for you special but I said that was hardly the point the point was if a business has succeeded by offering a satisfying product then oughtn't it behoove the business to continue to offer that product as long as the customer shows enthusiasm for it? Doesn't seem like good business. Doesn't make sense to me but then maybe I have become irrelevant. Maybe that is the lesson I'm to learn. The lesson of my own irrelevance. Perhaps that's it. My obsolescence.

[*Pause.*]

But they made the salad for me and it was tasty. As it always has been. And we have our health.

[*Pause.*]

Then when I got back to the office there was quite a controversy as two men from the contractor's had arrived to install the new commode next to the vestry. Now, the pastor had been absolutely clear that the model he had requested was a silent flush model but these two gentlemen were in adamant disagreement. So I produced the paperwork and said gentlemen you have been confronted with the evidence of your mistake and I will not allow you to compound it by proceeding. And with the help of the custodian I blocked their way. The vulgarity of the language. As he drove me home the pastor said thank you, Grace, another crisis narrowly averted.

[*Pause.*]

But I do hope they put that salad back on the menu.

[*Pause.*]

Well, perhaps I'll see about making that sandwich.

[*She does not move.*]

Have you been drinking today, dear?

CARLA: No. I haven't.

GRACE: You haven't.

CARLA: But I appreciate you asking.

GRACE: I had hoped we were past that.

CARLA: We are.

GRACE: Since the hospital.

CARLA: We're past it, Grace.

GRACE: All right, then.

CARLA: All right, then.

GRACE: You know when Gene died I felt for quite some time that I wouldn't be able to go on. I did. Yet here I am. I know you don't think so right now but you will feel better someday. I think I have enough experience to say this.

[Pause.]

So perhaps those two young men were here today.

CARLA: What two young men?

GRACE: I can't remember their *names*.

CARLA: Chet and Gibby?

GRACE: From Fourth of July.

CARLA: Why would you think they were here?

GRACE: I don't think I was ever introduced.

CARLA: What would they be doing here?

GRACE: I don't know, dear. You're the one who is friendly with them.

CARLA: They're friends of Thor's.

GRACE: In a sense.

CARLA: They happen to like Thor.

GRACE: And they like you as well.

[Pause.]

CARLA: Grace.

GRACE: I was an attractive woman at one time.

CARLA: Okay, Grace.

GRACE: I know that may be difficult to picture. But I don't want you to think that I don't understand what it is like. I *do* understand.

CARLA: Thor met them at the *pool*. They work at the *pool*.

GRACE: Yes, it's nice for him to make some friends.

CARLA: They taught him how to do a backflip.

GRACE: But if I remember correctly the day that they were here before, Thor spent the evening watching television with me while they smoked and drank outside on the patio with you.

CARLA: Grace.

GRACE: And I'm not entirely sure what benefit he derived from that. In fact, as I recall, they were here long after Thor went to sleep.

CARLA: We . . . *talked*. I . . . I . . . I honestly don't know why I'm having to . . . I liked *talking* to them, we were . . . I don't know why I am *justifying* having *talked* to a couple of . . .

GRACE: I'm simply trying to understand.

CARLA: I mean who am I going to *talk* to, Grace? Who do you expect me to talk to? In the course of a day. Who do I talk to? I'm asking you. Honestly. Who? Honestly. You tell me.

GRACE: *We're* talking, aren't we?

[*Pause.*]

CARLA: In answer to your question, no. They were not here today.

GRACE: Well. I thought I would ask.

CARLA: Okay.

GRACE: Because I found this in your laundry hamper.

[*She pulls a vodka bottle out of the basket.*]

And so I made that assumption.

CARLA: *I'm* going to do the laundry.

GRACE: Well, we also seem to be out of detergent.

CARLA: No we're not.

GRACE: I think so.

CARLA: There's a brand-new box.

GRACE: I didn't see one.

CARLA: Right on top of the machine.

GRACE: I don't think so, but . . .

CARLA: Did you *look*? You must not have looked.

GRACE: I did, but . . .

CARLA: Follow me. I'll show you exactly where it is.

GRACE: I believe you.

CARLA: But you're implying that I forgot to get detergent.

GRACE: No. I didn't say that.

CARLA: And the fact of the matter is that I *did.*

GRACE: All right, then. But . . .

CARLA: It's a bright orange box. It's impossible to miss it.

GRACE: But since your young men drank *beer* that night, rather than liquor, the beer that has been sitting all this time in our refrigerator, and since this bottle is half empty, I thought you might know where it came from.

[*Pause.*]

CARLA: Wouldn't it be nicer to say it's half *full*?

GRACE: Have you been drinking today?

[THOR *appears.*]

THOR: It's mine.

CARLA: Go away.

GRACE: This is a private conversation, Thor.

THOR: I drank it.

CARLA: Don't.

GRACE: It's not polite to eavesdrop on a private conversation.

THOR: I just walked in and you were talking.

GRACE: All right.

THOR: Why is it private?

GRACE: We can talk about that later.

THOR: I have to talk to Mom.

GRACE: After we're done, Thor.

THOR: When will that be?

CARLA: Get your little ass out of here.

GRACE: Oh, no. Oh, no, dear. Really. Dear. Not the language.

THOR: I like vodka.

[*Pause.*]

GRACE [*to* THOR]: If it's yours, where did you get it?

THOR: Liquor store.

GRACE: I see. And you drank half of this bottle?

THOR: Yeah.

GRACE: When was this?

THOR: Today.

GRACE: Today.

THOR: Yeah.

GRACE: You went to the liquor store today.

THOR: Yeah.

GRACE: While your mother was here.

THOR: She was asleep.

[*A high-pitched whistling sound begins.* THOR *and* CARLA *cover their ears.* GRACE *is oblivious.*]

GRACE: What liquor store was this?

CARLA: Grace.

GRACE: Because tomorrow you and I can go back there and talk to the proprietor.

CARLA: *Grace.*

GRACE: And we can ask him why he's selling . . . *What?*

CARLA: Batteries, Grace.

GRACE: What? You need to enunciate, dear.

THOR: *Batteries. Batteries.*

CARLA: *The batteries.*

GRACE: I don't know what that is. I've never heard of a *paddery.*

THOR: *Turn it down turn it down turn it down . . .*

CARLA: *Batteries, Grace. The batteries in the thing.*

[*She points to her ear.*]

THOR [*continuously*]: *. . . turn it down turn it down turn it down turn it down . . .*

GRACE: Thor. We don't need to sh—Oh. I see.

[*She adjusts the volume. The whistling stops.*]

If you feel compelled to *shout,* you can go outside.

[*The doorbell rings. No one moves.* CARLA *sits. Then* GRACE *sits. Then* THOR. *It rings again.* THOR *goes to answer it. After twenty seconds or so, he returns.*]

THOR [*to* CARLA]: A guy wants to talk to you.

CARLA [*groaning*]: What guy?

THOR: I don't know.

GRACE [*to* CARLA]: Were you expecting someone?

CARLA: Who would I be expecting?

GRACE: What is his name?

THOR: I don't know.

GRACE: Did you ask?

THOR: No.

GRACE: Did he say what he wanted?

THOR: To see Mom.

GRACE: Why, I mean?

CARLA: Why do you *think*?

THOR: No.

GRACE: He didn't say?

CARLA: To *console* me.

GRACE: What sort of man?

CARLA: To bring me another *casserole*.

THOR: An army guy.

CARLA: Say I'm sick.

[THOR *goes. Pause.*]

GRACE: I would *hope,* were the shoe on the other foot and *you* had made the effort . . .

CARLA: *What?*

GRACE: I understand your irritation with *me.*

CARLA: What are you saying?

GRACE: Well. When someone goes out of their *way.*

CARLA: I'm in my *bathrobe.*

GRACE: You have a legitimate grievance with me. It's understandable.

CARLA: Grace. I . . . I . . . I . . . What is the *point* of that? Who uses words like "grievance"?

GRACE: It's not impolite to be *precise.*

CARLA: It's just . . . *when* . . . *how* did it become my responsibility . . .

GRACE [*overlapping*]: But to take it out on a person who has gone out of their way . . .

CARLA: . . . to entertain total *strangers*?

GRACE: . . . to make you an offer of kindness.

CARLA: Samaritans. Yes. I know.

GRACE: It could be, that is, it is possible that one might benefit from avoiding isolation.

CARLA: *Isolation?*

GRACE: It's possible.

CARLA: But how would I *know*? If I could *try* some isolation maybe we could find out.

[THOR *reenters.*]

GRACE: Yes, Thor?

THOR: He says his name is Purdy. He says it'll only take ten minutes.

CARLA [*rising and exiting toward the hallway*]: *Christ.* There was a time, you know, a time when people could take a subtle *hint.* When you didn't have to *spell it out.* Well, by all means. Bring him in. Bring 'em all in. Casserole for dinner tonight, Grace.

[*A door slams. She is gone.*]

GRACE: I'll make coffee.

[GRACE *goes into the kitchen.* THOR *exits. We hear a door close.* PURDY *enters.* THOR *follows.* PURDY *wears a corporal's uniform. His right hand is artificial.*]

THOR: Did you bring a casserole?

PURDY: A what?

THOR: Casserole.

PURDY: No.

[*Pause.* THOR *sits.* PURDY *sits.*]

THOR: Do you want a beer?

PURDY: No thank you, son.

THOR: We have some.

PURDY: No thank you.

THOR: You want a Coke?

PURDY: No thanks.

THOR: I drink beer sometimes.

PURDY: Okay.

THOR: You don't like the way it tastes?

PURDY: Tastes fine.

THOR: So why don't you drink it?

PURDY: Personal reasons.

THOR: What about whiskey?

PURDY: No.

THOR: What about vodka?

PURDY: No.

THOR: What about Kahlúa?

PURDY: No.

THOR: What about Andre's Cold Duck?

PURDY: No.

THOR: Are you religious?

PURDY: No.

[*Pause.*]

THOR: What about Harveys Bristol Cream?

PURDY: I'll have some coffee. If you have some coffee.

[THOR *stands and goes into the kitchen.* PURDY *sits and stares for almost a full minute.* THOR *returns and sits.*]

THOR: My grandmother's making it.

PURDY: Okay.

THOR: She said about five minutes.

PURDY: Sounds good.

[*Pause.*]

THOR: What happened to your hand?

PURDY: Buried ordnance.

THOR: Blew your hand off.

PURDY: Mm-hmm.

THOR: Is that a fake hand?

PURDY: Yep.

THOR: What's it made of?

PURDY: Fiberglass.

THOR: How does it stay on?

PURDY: Has a strap on it.

THOR: Leather strap.

PURDY: Uh-huh.

THOR: Where does the strap go?

PURDY: Around the forearm.

THOR: Why didn't you get one of those claws?

PURDY: Didn't like the way it looked.

THOR: But you could pick stuff up.

PURDY: I guess that's right.

[*Pause.*]

THOR: You want a magazine?

PURDY: No thanks.

[*Pause.* THOR *takes out the finger guillotine.*]

THOR: Put your finger in here.

PURDY: No thanks.

THOR: Why not?

PURDY: I'd just rather not.

THOR: Scared to.

PURDY: No.

THOR: Scared it'll chop your finger off.

PURDY: No.

THOR: So do it.

PURDY: I've seen how those work.

THOR: So?

PURDY: I'm not very interested in jokes and novelties.

[THOR *puts the guillotine away.*]

What grade you in?

THOR: Sixth.

PURDY: Make good grades?

THOR: Yeah.

PURDY: As and Bs?

THOR: Yeah.

PURDY: Not so hard, then.

THOR: Fuckin' easy.

PURDY: Okay.

[*Pause.*]

THOR: Do you know how to make a punji trap?

PURDY: No.

THOR: I want to know how deep a hole you have to dig.

PURDY: I don't know. Fairly deep, I suppose.

THOR: Do you have to make the spikes out of bamboo or could they just be wood spikes?

PURDY: Wood could probably do you just as well.

THOR: But it's not that hard to make.

PURDY: You may be right.

THOR: And then you shit on them.

PURDY: On the spikes.

THOR: For poison. So when you fall on the spikes you get poisoned by the shit.

PURDY: Hmm.

THOR: Think if you fell in. Like if you were standing over the hole shitting on the spikes and all of a sudden you were slipping and then you were like "whoa" and you fell in the hole with your pants down and died like that.

PURDY: I would imagine that the feces is applied before the sticks are planted in the trap rather than deposited from overhead.

[*Pause.*]

You mind checking on that coffee for me?

THOR [*at the top of his lungs*]: *Is the coffee ready?*

PURDY: How about if you go and check?

[THOR *stands and goes. Then he returns and sits.*]

THOR: Not yet.

PURDY: Okay.

[*Pause.*]

THOR: Do you know the capital of Greenland?

PURDY: No.

THOR: Godthåb.

PURDY: Huh.

THOR: Do you know the capital of Burundi?

PURDY: No.

THOR: Bujumbura.

PURDY: Huh.

THOR: Do you know the capital of Kentucky?

PURDY: Frankfort.

THOR: Most people say Louisville.

PURDY: It's Frankfort.

[*Pause.*]

THOR: Did you ever fuck any whores?

PURDY: Does your mother know you use that kind of language?

THOR: She taught me this language.

PURDY: No. I didn't.

THOR: Suckee suckee five buckee. My friend Ricky Purzer has a cousin in the Marines and he says there's all these whores and they always say suckee suckee five buckee.

PURDY: Your mother must be a very special person.

THOR: Hey G.I. Joe me love you long time.

PURDY: A very unique person.

THOR: My friend Ricky's cousin saw Andy Williams do a show.

PURDY: Okay.

THOR: Did you see that show?

PURDY: No.

THOR: And Flip Wilson and Nancy Sinatra.

PURDY: Huh.

THOR: And Tiny Tim from *Laugh-In*.

[*Pause.*]

> I think if you made a punji trap it'd have to be at least six feet deep because if you weren't falling fast enough the spikes wouldn't go in very far. This guy down the street Matt Cresap he has a Husqvarna and sometimes he takes the cap off the gas tank and he puts his cigarette out in the gas tank. But the reason it doesn't blow up is because it's only the vapors that blow up and if you do it really fast the vapors don't blow up and it just goes out like *pfffft*. And all the little kids are like running away 'cause they're so scared it's gonna explode. I figured out how to make jelly gas. If you take Styrofoam you know the kind that they have at like a flower shop and you put it in gasoline it dissolves and turns into jelly gas and you can light it and throw it and it explodes. I made a flamethrower too with a can of hair spray.

[*Pause.*]

Did you ever eat dog meat?

PURDY: The *flesh* of a dog?

THOR: Yeah.

PURDY: No.

THOR: But people do.

PURDY: What people?

THOR: Where you were.

PURDY: It's possible.

THOR: All the time.

PURDY: I don't know.

THOR: They love it. Barbecued dog.

PURDY: Hmm.

THOR: I would eat dog.

PURDY: Okay.

THOR: To stay alive. Think if you were starving.

PURDY: Sure.

THOR: You'd have to. People say they wouldn't but they all would if they had to.

PURDY: Maybe so.

THOR: You wouldn't have a choice. But people over there don't eat it because they have to. They like it. They do. It's their favorite thing.

PURDY: I wouldn't know.

THOR: Suckee suckee five buckee. [*With a Chinese accent*] Ah-so. Me rike more dog meat, prease.

[*Pause.*]

You never saw that? People eating a dog?

PURDY: No.

THOR: Oh.

[*Long pause.*]

PURDY: I did see a dog eat a *person.*

[GRACE *enters with coffee, a slice of cake, and a fork. At the sound of her voice,* THOR *starts to leave.*]

GRACE: Yoo-hoo. Here we are then. Thor?

THOR [*stopping*]: What?

GRACE: Are you going to move that ladder?

THOR: I don't predict the future.

[THOR *goes.*]

GRACE [*to* PURDY]: I don't trust that ladder. Well. Isn't this a treat? I always say there's nothing quite so nice as an unexpected guest. Always a treat.

PURDY: Thank you, ma'am.

GRACE: Lars had so many friends. I always knew that he was popular with his crowd but I have to say, Mr. Birney, it has been a bit overwhelming to see just how true that was. Do you take sugar?

PURDY: Black, please.

GRACE: There's also a bit of cake. Do you like cake?

PURDY: Not for me.

GRACE: Do you know the Livelys? Marjorie Lively made it.

PURDY: No.

GRACE: Don and Marjorie Lively?

PURDY: No.

GRACE: I'm surprised. Well. You know, my father loved entertaining. He was *convivial*. My mother, on the other hand, was retiring by nature. She was ill for much of her life. I would offer you milk but it seems we had a bit of miscommunication about the market. [*Realizing*] Oh dear. You did say *black* quite clearly, didn't you?

PURDY: Either way.

GRACE: The sweet one will be for me, then. The sweeter the better. [*Pouring*] Here we go, then. Black as midnight, as Lars would say.

PURDY: It's *Purdy*.

GRACE: Beg pardon?

PURDY [*pointing to his name tag*]: *Purdy*. Rather than *Birney*.

GRACE: Oh my. Gracious. Do you know, I spend a *king's ransom* on batteries for this device.

PURDY: It's all right.

GRACE: The world can get *cacophonous*. But as the world turns *up* its volume, nature has done me the favor of turning mine *down*.

PURDY: What did she suffer from?

GRACE: Whom?

PURDY: Your mother was ill, you said.

GRACE: Oh. She was born with her internal organs reversed.

PURDY: Really?

GRACE: Yes.

PURDY: Is that right?

GRACE: Oh yes.

PURDY: Reversed?

GRACE: Mm-hmm.

PURDY: That's unusual.

GRACE: Extremely.

PURDY: This was a diagnosis?

GRACE: Oh yes.

PURDY: Reversed left to right?

GRACE: Yes.

PURDY: Huh. [*Thinks.*] Would that make a *difference*?

GRACE: Apparently it does. She was by no means convivial. When did you arrive home?

PURDY: Very recently.

GRACE: I don't know how you do it. The lack of routine. I couldn't. Lars was well suited, though. Never one to complain. Like my father. How long had you known each other?

PURDY: Known whom?

GRACE: Oh. You probably knew him as Whitey. Towheaded as a boy, you know. Straw colored later on but somehow the name stuck.

PURDY: So Lars was also known as Whitey.

GRACE: Whitey Larsen. Although my daughter-in-law tells me that the name may have gained an unfortunate *racial* connotation.

PURDY: Whitey? Could be.

GRACE: How sad the way innocent things can get twisted. I have to tell you, I don't envy young people. What a difficult time to be young. With the anger and the vulgarity and the controversy. It was very different for me. Back in the *dark ages*. My father would always say if you can't say something nice don't say anything at all and of course I bristled at that back then but as time goes on the wisdom of that advice becomes more apparent.

PURDY: If you can't say something *nice*.

GRACE: Yes.

PURDY: Of course that might lead to the occasional extended period of *silence*.

GRACE: I don't think silence is anything to be afraid of.

[*Extended period of silence.* GRACE *grows afraid.* CARLA *enters. She has dressed with minimal care.*]

[*Relieved*] Oh. Well, then. Here we are. Dear, this is Corporal *Purdy*. I believe I've got that right now, haven't I?

PURDY: Yes, ma'am. Hello.

GRACE: Want to make sure. Had a bit of silliness with the name. I'm still red in the face.

PURDY: Doesn't matter.

GRACE: My mind is like an old lawn mower. Takes a few *pulls* to get it started.

PURDY [*to* CARLA]: I'm sorry. I should have called.

GRACE: Not at all.

PURDY: It being the dinner hour.

GRACE: On another occasion I would ask you to join us.

PURDY: No thank you.

GRACE: But on another occasion.

PURDY [*to* CARLA]: I . . . I understand that you're not feeling well.

CARLA: I'm fine.

PURDY: Oh. Good.

CARLA: No, you see, it's just that I'm a *drunk*.

[*Pause.*]

GRACE: Dear.

CARLA: I'm a drunk and I've been passed out on that sofa all day.

GRACE: Dear.

CARLA: No, it's true. Apparently I have a terrible drinking problem.

GRACE: There's just no need.

CARLA: And I'm also, it seems, a *prostitute*. A drunkard and a prostitute. But thank you for the coffee, Grace.

GRACE: Dear.

CARLA: What sort of casserole did you bring us?

PURDY: There . . . there seems to be some confusion on this matter of a *casserole*.

[*Silence.*]

GRACE: Mr. Purdy, did you know that it takes sixteen muscles to frown and only two to smile?

PURDY: Huh.

[*A timer rings offstage.*]

GRACE: Oh dear. The oven. Preheating it. Yes. I'll come back.

[*She goes.*]

CARLA: Sorry.

PURDY: No.

CARLA: Yes.

PURDY: No. I'll go.

CARLA: No. Sit.

PURDY: No. It was . . . *remiss* of me . . .

CARLA: No. It's very kind.

PURDY: Nonetheless.

CARLA: No. I'm serious. Sit.

PURDY: No. I'm sometimes not the best judge of these situations.

CARLA: No. Well, who *is*?

PURDY: So I have to rely on your . . . candor.

CARLA: I'm trying to say.

PURDY: No, because if you are being . . . if you are simply indulging me . . .

CARLA: I'm very sorry.

PURDY: Then there's really no point.

CARLA: No. But you have to understand that after a certain amount of time . . .

PURDY: No. I understand.

CARLA: There's only so much *grief* that a person can . . . can . . . you know . . .

PURDY: Yes.

CARLA: I don't know, *ingest.*

PURDY: Yes.

CARLA: So if I come off seeming like some sort of insupportable *cunt* and—well fantastic now I've managed to work the word "cunt" into a sentence within three minutes of meeting you.

PURDY: I know the word.

CARLA: And these *grief casseroles* . . . Do you need a casserole dish? Really, take all you need.

PURDY: No.

CARLA: There's a line around the block. I swear to God, a long line, all these long faces, all these *vultures* with oven mitts and Tupperware converging on the house. *Vulture* casserole is what they should call it.

PURDY: Right.

CARLA: Not to be cold blooded about it, but . . . *show's over.* All right? Go *home.* Remember *life?* Remember *living people?* [*Sighs.*] Lars's commander and his wife were here three weeks ago to present the medal, and *Grace,* well, you've had the pleasure of meeting Grace.

PURDY: Yes.

CARLA: And there's a photographer to, I suppose, *record* the event for posterity and I politely *decline,* you know, I'd honestly rather not have to smile for the camera as I'm being handed this morbid little piece of *jewelry,* but Grace, you met Grace, God bless her, she's *right there.* She's on *top* of it, bless her little heart. They say then how about we get a shot of his mother and I tell you Grace pops up like she's just won a game of *bingo,* she's standing by the fireplace with the other *vampires* and they're checking the light with one of those meters and Grace suddenly makes a little noise, a little *squeak* like a little *prairie dog,* and she pulls out a mirror and touches up her *lipstick.* And what a valuable lesson. No matter how difficult the situation, you can always *look your best.*

[*Pause.*]

So you'll understand if I'm not quite as gracious as I should be.

PURDY: You don't remember me, do you?

[*Long pause.*]

CARLA: No, of course. No, I . . . of course I . . .

PURDY: It's all right.

CARLA: No, wait . . . I . . . Remind me?

PURDY: From the hospital.

CARLA: Ohhhh. Yes.

PURDY: It's all right.

CARLA: You . . . you're . . . the *chaplain?*

PURDY: No.

CARLA: Wait a minute.

PURDY: Don't worry.

CARLA: I think that I . . .

PURDY: I would honestly be surprised if you did.

CARLA: The military hospital?

PURDY: It's okay.

CARLA: When are you talking about?

PURDY: July.

CARLA: Well. I mean . . .

PURDY: We talked one day.

CARLA: I was . . . *there.* In July.

PURDY: Same time as me.

CARLA: Right. And . . . we talked?

PURDY: I . . . *didn't,* really. *You* talked about . . . snakes.

CARLA: No. Wait. I'm talking about the Twenty-third at Fort Irwin.

PURDY: I remember it very clearly.

[*Pause.* CARLA *shakes her head.*]

CARLA [*gently*]: I . . . don't think so.

PURDY: You had a white bathrobe with blue flowers.

CARLA: *Snakes?*

PURDY: Three snakes. That come out of a jar.

CARLA: I . . . I . . . no . . .

PURDY: I didn't fully understand the significance. I thought you might remember.

CARLA: Hmm-mm. No.

PURDY: Doesn't matter.

CARLA: I wish I did.

PURDY: Presumptuous of me to think.

CARLA: You came to visit *me.* In the hospital.

PURDY: I was there myself.

[*Pause.*]

I lost my hand.

[*He shows her.*]

Here.

[CARLA *gasps, then begins to laugh.*]

CARLA: Oh! Oh my God. I . . . I'm sorry. Ouch. Jesus. I didn't even . . .
   Lost it? Oops. Don't you remember where you *put it?*

PURDY: I know, it's . . .

CARLA [*embarrassed*]: God. I'm sorry. That's . . . it's . . .

PURDY: It's a little creepy.

CARLA: No.

PURDY: Maybe.

CARLA: Maybe a little.

PURDY: It's fiberglass.

CARLA: I didn't even notice.

PURDY: It's nice of you to say that.

CARLA: I didn't.

PURDY: Purely cosmetic. Which you might take as a measure of my personal vanity. Still, the best of several unappealing options. And you can bend the fingers. To various positions.

CARLA: And how did it . . . ?

PURDY: Buried ordnance.

CARLA: I see.

PURDY: Stupid mistake. One among many.

CARLA: It's really only the color that's noticeable.

PURDY: Not a perfect match, no.

CARLA: No. It's a little . . .

PURDY: Swarthy, yes. The choices were limited. I've thought of painting it. To even things out.

CARLA: That might work.

PURDY: Unfortunately, *being* right handed . . .

CARLA: *Oops.*

PURDY: Bit of a challenge.

CARLA: Yes.

PURDY: But. When my dexterity improves. With the left.

CARLA: That's funny. I could never play the piano *before.*

PURDY: What's that?

CARLA: Nothing.

PURDY: I don't understand.

CARLA: That old joke.

PURDY: Don't know it.

CARLA: Never mind.

PURDY: No, please.

CARLA: It's terrible . . . it's . . . a man loses his hands and the doctor sews them back on and after the surgery the man says Doctor will I be able to play the piano when I recover and the doctor says I don't see why not and the man says that's funny I could never . . . you know . . . play the piano . . . before. Terrible joke.

PURDY: Actually, I *did* play the piano. But I can see the humor in that.

[*Pause.*]

So you don't remember me.

CARLA: Maybe your face.

PURDY: Right.

CARLA: You have to understand, there are a couple of days for which I can't . . .

PURDY: Account.

CARLA: With the medication. And everything. So it would be a little surprising.

PURDY: If you did. Remember.

CARLA: I'm sorry.

PURDY: You asked me to untie your hands.

CARLA: Oh.

PURDY: We were talking. *You* were talking, I suppose is the way to say it. And you said once the snakes are out of the jar how do you get them back in? And you said could you untie my hands?

CARLA: They were, yes.

PURDY: They're trying to kill me you said. And I said I didn't think that was right. I said that no one was going to hurt you, that you were perfectly safe as far as I could tell, so I said I can't do that for you, that I wished I could but that they didn't want you to hurt yourself, so I thought it wasn't my place to do that. You looked at me. I couldn't tell if you really saw me. I said I thought I should call the doctor and you said go fuck yourself. Then you said I'll hate you for as long as you live. Then I left the room.

[*Long silence.*]

CARLA: You see, no one ever bothers to tell you that a military transport isn't going to have a *beverage service.* Whoever heard of a seven-hour flight without any sort of *reasonably stocked beverage service*? Fucking military. No wonder Lars had a stick up his ass. Sorry. He's your friend. But yes, when you've been on a plane for seven hours without the beverage service and they set you down in the middle of some *desert,* in *July,* and they say to you we'll need to get things under way as soon as we can so go ahead and relax, get four hours of sleep, go ahead, we just need to get things started at the chapel at oh-nine-hundred but if there's anything you need, you let us know, and you say well you know since you bring it up there might be one little thing actually I'm just a little parched you know just something to take some of the edge off is that the sort of thing that one might be able to find at three in the morning in the middle of this godforsaken wasteland and then of course the embarrassed looks as you realize that, oops, you happen to be talking to the fucking *chaplain.* Would it be too much to sport the traditional collar so that a person doesn't make a complete *jackass* of herself? So nine A.M. And you've spent the night next to the ice-cold window unit thinking gee remember how every time Lars would come home from a tour how he'd spend the first week showing you everything that you'd done wrong in the house? Tugging on the pleats of those curtains, down on his hands and knees with a comb, a black rubber pocket comb *combing the fringe* on that rug gotta get the *fringe* straight gotta maintain that *fringe* at ninety degrees look sharp there, carpet. You know, Carla, you know, baby, all it takes is a little attention to detail, walking around in his Jockey shorts whistling "The Halls of Montezuma." So. Nine A.M. And they take you to this little room and now you're really starting to feel like you could use that beverage, you know, you've really hit the point where a little nail polish, a little hair spray, might just do the trick, a little Windex maybe but no, they take you to the room and you want to say *Larsen,* you pathetic morons *Larsen* don't you know a Lutheran name when you see one for Christ's sake how stupid do you have to be? *Larsen. No open casket in the Lutheran church.* Consult one of your many manuals. This *is* my *husband* here, all right? This *is* the piece of shit himself here in this aluminum box this display case who used to hit me across the face with a rolled-up newspaper like you hit a dog this embalmed asshole who used to do this to me in front of our *child* could we grant him please his privacy and close the fucking *lid?* And then they hand you this plastic bag this see-through vinyl pouch for your entertainment little packet of nostalgia down memory lane with his Timex watch and the pocketknife and the cheap J. C. Penney *wallet* and you're thinking well as long as there's a lull, a little break in the action maybe *I'm* in here somewhere, maybe tucked away here in the back behind the credit cards, me and Thor, maybe, hey Lars how's the wife and kids well lemme show ya but now wait a minute, hang on here, funny, I don't recall *this* event this particular *Kodak moment* with the little slanty-eyed girl on my husband's lap what is she fourteen fifteen with all the mascara it's hard to tell wearing nothing but sequins and glue and a smile right there on his lap in the little high heels legs crossed and he's giving the photographer the big thumbs up with one hand while the other squeezes the little yellow titty that he is *licking. Or* maybe she spilled her drink and he's helping clean her off because he's such a thoughtful man, your husband, the same man who has refused to fuck *you* for the last two years because you're too *disgusting* to fuck, he says, you smell like a distillery. Who in their right mind would want to fuck you? What happened you used to make an effort you used to have a little pride and I say well you certainly know how to charm the ladies big boy, you certainly know how to make a woman feel special so when you see this poor little fifteen-year-old whore in a miniskirt sitting on the lap of your dead husband the prick laid out in a tin can at the other end of the room, *well.* When you're looking at that and you've been wanting a drink for the past twenty-four hours, thirty-six when you factor in the day spent packing, with your son trying to figure out how to mourn the man who used to give him a bloody nose if he tracked mud in the house, I mean, when you add all that up, I guess it's not unreasonable to assume that something had to give.

[*Pause.* THOR *comes down the hallway wearing a werewolf mask and hands. He passes through and exits toward the kitchen.*]

PURDY: I'm sorry that he passed away.

CARLA: Thank you.

PURDY: And for your son. That's *Thor?*

CARLA: Yes.

PURDY: For him, too.

[*From the kitchen, we hear a crash, and* GRACE *screams.* THOR *comes through the room again and exits to the hall.*]

May I make an observation? You seem to be the sort of person who has a lot of negative feelings about herself. You tend to feel like maybe you've done a lot of things wrong. Am I right about that?

CARLA [*shrugging*]: Possibly.

PURDY: I say this because until recently I had very negative thoughts about *myself*. I had begun to think that all of the things that I wanted, all of the things that I enjoyed, must be bad and that I must be a bad person for wanting them. It's hard to say exactly *why* I felt this way. I don't know. I never had a lot of friends, and my father would tell me, with some frequency, that I *was* a bad person. That I was selfish and greedy and thought only of myself, not of the other person, that I didn't take the feelings of others into consideration, and that made *me* a bad person. And naturally I believed him because he was my father and why would your father tell you something that wasn't true? I said to him how am I supposed to become a better person? How do I achieve that? And he said simply listen to your conscience. And I was confused. I said is my *conscience* the same as my *soul*? No, he said, your conscience is different. Your *conscience* is a little angel that sits right here on your shoulder and he tells you when you have done something bad. It's sitting there right now. It never goes to sleep and it never gets tired. I see. So I said what if you want to do something even though your conscience says not to? And he said that's what we call wickedness. But I said what if the conscience makes a mistake? What if it takes over and it makes you feel bad about everything that you love? Everything perfect or beautiful? And he said it never makes a mistake. Ever? Never, he said. He said think about this: Why do you think that people who set a building on fire always come back to the scene of the crime? Why would they do that? They don't *want* to go to *jail*, do they? No, their *conscience* makes them come back. He said their conscience knows it was wrong, and it has a little tiny whip, and it whips them and whips them until they go back to that burning building to see how wicked they were. And I thought about this for a few seconds. I really had to think. That didn't seem right. I thought very hard about it and after a few seconds I turned to him and I said . . .

CARLA: They go back because the burning building is beautiful.

PURDY: Yes. That's exactly what I said. I didn't get my allowance that week.

[*They both smile and stare at the floor.* PURDY *laughs.*]

CARLA: What?

PURDY: That's funny. I could never play the piano *before*.

[*Pause. They smile and begin laughing for a bit.*]

What an astonishing volume of horseshit people expect you to swallow. Do you know what I mean? What a staggering, towering load of pure unreconstituted crap, delivered to your door every day by everyone you know, all these respectable citizens trundling up to your front door with their enormous creaking carts full of shit, each one with a blindfold and a clothespin on their nose, each one deluded, each one *narcotized* into thinking that they are, in fact, hauling an equal quantity of *diamonds*. And each one offering you a little spoonful of the stuff. A spoonful of their precious horseshit. Go ahead. Have a taste. Today's your lucky day. With each spoonful you get a free cartload. Free mountain of shit. Shit *volcano*. C'mon. Dig in. Doesn't taste like shit. I swear. Tastes great. Tastes like diamonds and rubies and pimento cheese and comfy sofas and football games and beer and rock and roll and *Playboy* magazine and *The Tonight Show* and *Hollywood Squares* and Hallmark cards and little sayings in needlepoint on their pillows and art museums and the theater and church on Sunday. And you can shape the horseshit into any shape you want, any shape at all, it's very elastic. But when you pop it in your mouth and swallow it down, it still comes out horse-shit. And not a one of them, not a *one*, has the courage to unbuckle their harness and leave their horseshit behind for two seconds and experience a single uninterrupted moment of genuine beauty.

CARLA: I'm not really sure I have any idea what it is you're talking about. But I'm almost certain that I agree with it.

PURDY: I'm trying to say that it might be a good idea for you not to blame yourself so much. That's what I decided. A few years ago I decided to take that little conscience, the one that my father said had been sitting on my shoulder all those years, sitting there with his little whip, I decided to take that conscience off my shoulder and snap its neck, just like a little sparrow's neck. I think you might feel better if you did the same thing.

[*Pause.*]

CARLA: Maybe you should stay for dinner.

PURDY: That would be nice.

[THOR *enters on his way to the kitchen.*]

CARLA [*to* THOR]: Hey.

THOR: Hey what?

CARLA: That clock is crooked.

[THOR *climbs the ladder and begins straightening the clock.*]

You're sort of different from most of Lars's friends.

PURDY: Is that good or bad?

CARLA: I don't know.

PURDY: How would you characterize his friends?

CARLA: I . . . well, I don't . . . It's sort of difficult to . . . In *general,* and I'm not including you in this, but in *general* I guess I'd have to characterize them as . . . as . . . *generally* a bunch of *motherfucking assholes.*

[*They laugh and smile. And then suddenly the ladder is falling over with* THOR *on it.*]

PURDY: Hey! *Hey!! Look out! Look out!!*

CARLA [*simultaneously*]: Thor! *Thor!! Careful, Thor!!!*

[PURDY *springs from the sofa and without thinking reaches out to* THOR *with his false hand.* THOR *grabs for it as he falls and pulls it, strap and all, off* PURDY's *arm.* CARLA *screams again.* THOR *hits the ground and realizes what he is holding. He screams and throws the hand on the sofa.* GRACE *rushes in.* CARLA *sees the hand and begins to laugh uncontrollably at* THOR's *distress. The following three lines are more or less simultaneous, with ad-libs.*]

THOR [*screaming at* CARLA]: Shut up! It's not funny! Shut up, you stupid cow! Shut up shut up shut up, you disgusting pig! Quit it!! I don't know why you're laughing, because it's NOT FUNNY!!! SHUT UP!!!

GRACE: I told you, Thor, I told you *several times* that this is what could happen, but you chose not to listen to me and now just look. Thor! Not so loud!

PURDY [*to* GRACE]: I'm sorry, ma'am. The boy was on the ladder, and I thought I was helping, but apparently I just complicated the situation.

[PURDY *retrieves his hand from the sofa.* CARLA *cannot stop laughing. She holds her stomach, puts her hand to her mouth, looks around, and* quickly grabs a wastebasket. *She throws up into it, which is to say, she turns downstage and we see the vomit come out of her mouth. The others see this. Pause.*]

GRACE: Thor, could you take that ladder out, please?

THOR: Why?

GRACE: Thor.

THOR: Why do I have to do it?

GRACE: I warned you something like this might happen.

PURDY: I'll do it.

GRACE [*to* PURDY]: I think it's probably time we said good night.

PURDY: Uh. All right.

GRACE: It was so kind of you to go out of your way like this.

PURDY: You're very welcome.

GRACE: We're just about to sit down to dinner.

PURDY: Right.

GRACE: But it was so nice to meet you.

PURDY: Yes.

GRACE: If you're ever this way again . . .

PURDY: I will.

GRACE: I hope so.

PURDY: I definitely will.

GRACE: Good.

PURDY: Definitely.

GRACE: Good. So . . .

[*He doesn't move.*]

CARLA: Could somebody get me a glass of water?

PURDY: Uh . . .

GRACE: Thor?

THOR [*to* GRACE]: I'm not your *slave*.

[*Pause.* THOR *goes to the kitchen.*]

GRACE [*to* PURDY]: Good night.

PURDY: I hope I didn't . . .

GRACE: You've been very kind.

PURDY: No, because I truly . . . I feel . . . perhaps . . . some *responsibility* . . .

GRACE: No.

PURDY: It being the dinner hour and all.

GRACE: Everything's fine.

[CARLA *feels another small wave of nausea. She picks up the wastebasket and exits up the hall.*]

PURDY [*to* GRACE]: Good night.

[*He exits. After a few seconds,* THOR *returns with a glass of water. He sees that* CARLA *has gone. He sets the water down and picks up the ladder, but rather than take it away, he sets it up again. He begins to climb it.*]

GRACE: No. No. Thor, no. Don't do that. No. No, Thor. I'm very serious now. I mean it. Don't go up there. Thor. *Thor.*

[*He reaches the clock and makes the tiniest adjustment in its angle.*]

All right, then. Thank you.

[THOR *comes down, folds the ladder, and carries it out of the room. After a moment,* CARLA *enters.*]

CARLA: Do you have the milk of magnesia?

GRACE: Why don't you lie down?

CARLA: Maybe I will.

GRACE: I think you should.

CARLA: Do we have any crackers?

GRACE: I may have eaten the last of them. There's bread.

[CARLA *shakes her head. Pause.*]

How is Dr. Wilborn's leg doing?

CARLA: What?

GRACE: Dr. Wilborn.

CARLA: His *leg?*

GRACE: I wondered if he was still using the cane.

CARLA: I don't know.

GRACE: You remember that he had phlebitis.

CARLA: Oh. I forgot.

GRACE: That's why he had the cane.

CARLA: All right. Well, I didn't notice a cane.

GRACE: Perhaps it's improved.

CARLA: Not today anyway.

GRACE: But it's strange because I saw him at Kroger's yesterday and he *had* the cane.

[*Pause.*]

You didn't see Dr. Wilborn, did you?

CARLA [*appalled*]: *Yes.*

GRACE: I'm trying to be helpful.

CARLA: What an interesting *method* you've chosen.

GRACE: I'll pick up some crackers at the market tomorrow.

CARLA: I'm going to go.

GRACE: The pastor can take me. Rather than your visit.

CARLA: I'm fine.

GRACE: Well. Obviously not. All right. Crackers, milk, and butter. And laundry detergent.

[*Pause.*]

What about tampons? Shall I pick some up for you?

[CARLA *stares at her.*]

Do you need some? Or do you have enough?

CARLA: I have enough.

GRACE: Yes, I know.

CARLA: So why did you ask?

GRACE: Well, I've noticed that on average you buy a new box every two months or so. And for the last three months, I've noticed that the number of tampons in the box in your bathroom cupboard has remained constant.

CARLA: Has it?

GRACE: That's what I've noticed.

CARLA: Grace, I've got to tell you. This *melodrama* that you have cooked up, this *soap opera*, no, sorry, this *mystery novel* that you have concocted with me as the central character, well, look, we've all got to have a hobby, all right? I'm sure it's a creative outlet for you, for your smutty little imagination, but I've got to tell you one of the key things is you want to keep your plotline *plausible*, you know? You gotta keep your facts straight or your audience isn't gonna let you get away with it, you know, if it's over three months since your hero died and the hero's wife hadn't seen him for six months prior to that, see, they'd say, you know, the timeline just doesn't quite work, *unless*, wait a minute, see, I didn't realize. That's the genius of your version, Grace, you throw in a *miracle*, now that's a twist. That's a new one. Like the New Testament. How about if from *beyond the grave* the holy spirit of the dead husband pays a secret visit to the central character and no one believes her? I think you have really got something there, Grace, keep up the good work, and *no*, I don't know what's wrong with me, and *yes*, if you believe that, then you are losing your mind, and *no*, I don't need any *tampons*.

GRACE: Would you like me to call the young man for you? You'll have to tell me which one it was. I was never introduced. But he does have the right to know.

CARLA [*still calm*]: Your son liked to *fuck* prostitutes, Grace, not *marry* them.

GRACE: Lars would be so sad to hear you use that language.

CARLA: Good thing he died, then, rather than hear me say the word "fuck."

GRACE: Dear, you make me want to cry.

CARLA: Don't cry, Grace. Maybe he'll be *resurrected*.

GRACE: You like to be hurtful and that's because of the alcohol.

CARLA: Of course it is.

GRACE: And then to allow Thor to lie for you. I don't consider that loving your child.

[CARLA *picks up the glass of water and hurls it at the wall, breaking it. She picks up the fork. She pushes it against her neck.*]

CARLA: *HOW ABOUT IF I STAB MYSELF, GRACE??!! HOW ABOUT IF I DO THAT??!! HUH??!! IF I STAB MYSELF WOULD THAT POSSIBLY, FOR FUCK'S SAKE, POSSIBLY GET YOU FOR FIFTEEN MINUTES OFF MY GODDAMN BACK?? FIFTEEN MINUTES OF QUIET. IS THAT SO MUCH TO FUCKING AAAAASK!!!!????*

[*She flings the fork across the room. Silence.*]

GRACE: No one wants you to hurt yourself, dear. You know we don't want that.

[THOR *enters.*]

THOR: Are we still going to eat?

GRACE: Dinner's going to be a little late tonight.

THOR: I'm hungry.

GRACE: Why don't you have a nice bowl of cereal? Wouldn't you like that? You could take it to your room.

THOR: We don't have any milk.

[*Pause.* THOR *doesn't move.*]

GRACE: Your mother and I are having a conversation, Thor.

THOR: What about?

GRACE: That's not important.

THOR: Tell me.

GRACE: Thor.

THOR: Tell me.

GRACE: We don't give *orders*.

THOR: Tell me.

GRACE: Thor.

THOR: Tell me.

GRACE: No.

THOR: Tell me.

GRACE: I want you to stop now.

THOR: Tell me.

GRACE: No.

THOR: Tell me.

GRACE: Thor.

THOR: Tell me.

GRACE: You're behaving like a spoiled—

THOR [*suddenly bellowing*]: *TELL ME!!!*

[*Pause.*]

GRACE: All right, then. Your mother is going to have a child.

THOR: You're a liar.

GRACE: No.

THOR: Yes you are.

GRACE: You asked for the truth and I told you.

THOR: I hate you.

GRACE: I think you know we don't use the word "hate" in this house.

THOR: Oh so it's your house now.

GRACE: No.

THOR: How much did you pay for it?

GRACE: "Hate" is a very strong word.

THOR: What if I said I wish you were dead?

GRACE: Well.

[*Pause.*]

All right, then.

[*The lights fade to black.*]

ACT TWO

[*Five-thirty* A.M., *central standard time. The house is completely dark once again. A dog barks outside. After a few seconds,* CARLA *appears in silhouette in the hallway. She wears only her nightgown. She braces herself against the wall, apparently in pain. She slowly makes her way across the room and exits to the kitchen. A few more seconds go by before she reappears carrying a purse. She turns on a lamp, which illuminates only a tabletop and her face. She empties the entire contents of the purse onto the table. She opens two different drawers and closes them in quick succession. She goes to a closet and finds her coat, then feels around in the pockets. She opens a cabinet and pulls out a phone book. She tosses it aside and heads back toward the closet. At that moment,* GRACE *turns on another lamp. She is sitting in a chair across the room, wearing her bathrobe and yellow rubber gloves.* CARLA *freezes.*]

GRACE: I don't think you'll find it there.

CARLA: What?

GRACE: The Yellow Pages.

CARLA: Where?

GRACE: In the closet.

CARLA: Why would the Yellow Pages be in the closet?

GRACE: I don't think it would be.

CARLA: I'm not looking for the Yellow Pages.

GRACE: I was mistaken.

[*Pause. They stare at each other.*]

I startled you.

CARLA: No.

GRACE: I'm sorry.

CARLA: You didn't.

GRACE: I should have spoken sooner.

CARLA: I wasn't startled.

GRACE: To let you know.

CARLA: Know what?

GRACE: That I was sitting here.

CARLA: I don't care.

GRACE: As a courtesy.

CARLA: Sit wherever you want.

GRACE: I'm sorry.

CARLA: I wasn't startled.

GRACE: Because I noticed you looking in the cabinet.

CARLA: So?

GRACE: And the White Pages didn't seem to suit your needs.

CARLA: Why are you *awake*?

GRACE: Well, I suppose it was the coffee. Did you have coffee, too?

CARLA: No.

GRACE: That's a lesson. Never after six or seven. Let that be a *lesson* for me.

CARLA: Go back to sleep.

GRACE: Not *black* coffee. The absence of milk may have been a factor. Undiluted like that. But as we don't seem to own a *cow,* there it is.

CARLA: A *cow*?

GRACE: For the milk.

CARLA: What are you talking about?

GRACE: Cows make milk.

CARLA: Of course we don't own a *cow.*

GRACE: It was a joke, dear.

CARLA: I don't know why you'd *say* that.

GRACE: Because we were out of milk.

CARLA: I know that.

GRACE: It was said in *jest.*

CARLA: I know, but . . . I *know.*

GRACE: I know you do.

[*Pause.*]

You look pale.

CARLA: I'm tired.

GRACE: Couldn't you sleep?

CARLA: Why are you wearing those gloves?

GRACE: I did some cleaning.

CARLA: In the middle of the night?

GRACE: Since I was awake.

CARLA: All right.

GRACE: As long as I was awake, I thought I'd do a little cleaning. [*Thinks.*] Not the *middle* of the night, exactly.

CARLA: No.

GRACE: Rather than sit alone in the dark and do nothing.

CARLA: But you *were* sitting alone in the dark.

GRACE: I took a little break.

[*Pause.*]

I'm sorry I startled you.

CARLA: You *didn't.*

GRACE: I would be angry, too.

CARLA: I'm *not* angry.

GRACE: Well, consternated.

CARLA: *Frustrated.*

GRACE: Because you can't find the Yellow Pages?

CARLA: Because of this *conversation.*

GRACE: Because you're tired.

CARLA: I'm not tired.

GRACE: You said you were tired.

CARLA: No, I said . . . All right. Yes. I guess I am.

GRACE: I was looking for the Yellow Pages just the other day.

CARLA: Grace.

GRACE: It *is* frustrating. It seems to have gone missing.

CARLA: Grace. I am not looking for the Yellow Pages.

GRACE: All right.

CARLA: I am not.

GRACE: All right.

CARLA: Looking.

GRACE: All right.

CARLA: For the Yellow Pages.

GRACE: All right.

[CARLA *exits to the hallway. After a few seconds, she returns and stares at* GRACE.]

CARLA: I'm looking for my keys.

GRACE: Your house keys?

CARLA: My key ring with my keys on it.

GRACE: Your *car* keys, then.

CARLA: My *keys,* yes. My keys.

GRACE: Where did you want to go?

CARLA: Have you seen them?

GRACE: I don't think anywhere will be open at this hour of the morning. Where were you planning to go?

CARLA: The Stop 'n' Go.

GRACE: On K Street?

CARLA: They're not in my coat pocket.

GRACE: The Stop 'n' Go won't be open at this hour.

CARLA: They're open twenty-four hours.

GRACE: Not anymore. Not since the summer.

CARLA: Or the doughnut shop.

GRACE: To buy doughnuts?

CARLA: To buy milk. We need milk. They sell milk.

[*Pause.*]

GRACE: I have your car keys.

CARLA: Where were they?

GRACE: They were in your purse.

CARLA: You took them out of my purse.

GRACE: I was cleaning out the car.

CARLA: My car.

GRACE: Rather than sit idly in the dark.

CARLA: Did you find what you were looking for?

GRACE: I don't understand.

CARLA: In the course of your inspection.

GRACE: Dear.

CARLA: And where are my keys now?

GRACE: They're in my pocket.

[*Pause.*]

CARLA: I suppose you can anticipate my next question.

GRACE: Where did you need to go, dear?

[THOR *enters, in pajamas. He turns on the overhead lights.*]

THOR: Does the post office have to pay you if they lose your mail?

GRACE: Thor.

THOR: They should have to pay you.

GRACE: It's too early.

THOR: So they just steal from you and you can't do anything about it?

GRACE: Please go back to sleep.

[CARLA *begins to search through several drawers. They watch her.*]

THOR: What's going on?

GRACE: You're going to be very tired if you don't go back to sleep.

THOR: So are you.

GRACE: Please. As a favor to me.

THOR: You first.

[CARLA *exits up the hallway, slamming a door as she goes.*]

What's she looking for?

GRACE: The Yellow Pages.

THOR: We don't have one.

GRACE: Of course we do.

THOR: Not anymore.

GRACE: What happened to it?

THOR: I used it for something.

GRACE: For what?

THOR: I burned it.

GRACE: Why?

THOR: For a fire.

GRACE: Where?

THOR: In the fireplace.

GRACE: Why didn't you turn up the thermostat?

THOR: Fires are nicer.

GRACE: But we have logs for that purpose.

THOR: Yellow Pages are free.

GRACE: But we need the Yellow Pages.

THOR: But I saved you money.

GRACE: I think you're making this up.

THOR: I don't care.

GRACE: You know the difference between right and wrong. You're not a child.

THOR: Yes I am.

[*Pause.*]

GRACE: You know, when people try to be hurtful to others, they usually wind up hurting themselves.

THOR: They must not plan very carefully.

[*There is a crash offstage.*]

CARLA [*from offstage*]: *. . . is there no motherfucking YELLOW PAGES IN THIS MOTHERFUCKING HOUSE!?!?!?*

GRACE: Back to bed now.

THOR: I'm not sleepy.

GRACE: I'm not discussing it.

THOR: Why is everyone awake?

[CARLA *reenters, quite agitated.*]

CARLA [*to* THOR]: Have you seen the extra keys?

THOR: What extra keys?

CARLA: On the metal ring.

THOR: No.

CARLA: They were in that drawer.

THOR: Why are you asking me?

CARLA: Did you move them?

THOR: I didn't know they existed.

CARLA: *They're on a metal ring.*

THOR: So blame *me.*

[CARLA *exits again.*]

Where's she going?

GRACE: No one is going anywhere.

THOR: There's nowhere open to go.

[CARLA *returns.*]

CARLA: Give me the keys, Grace.

GRACE: I would think that, at this point, the two of us could be more honest with each other.

CARLA: I want my keys.

GRACE: You tell me that you are going to the doughnut shop . . .

CARLA: No, you're right. You caught me. It's true. I'm going to get gasoline. A gallon of gas and a book of matches, and when the two of you go to sleep I'm going to pour the gasoline around your beds and set you both on fire.

GRACE: Thor?

THOR: What?

GRACE: Come here a moment.

THOR: You just told me to go away.

GRACE: Sit down here, please.

THOR: Fine with me.

[THOR *sits near* GRACE.]

GRACE: I want to tell you something. And I want you to know that I'm telling you this because I think that you are mature enough to understand. I'm not going to give the car keys to your mother because I believe that she has a drinking problem. Do you understand what that means?

THOR: *No hablo inglés.*

[CARLA *laughs and exits to the kitchen. Banging noises are heard.*]

GRACE: Yes. And I'm fairly certain that she wants the car keys so that she can go and find herself some more liquor. But I think that if I was to give her the car keys, that I would be helping her to hurt herself, and I don't think that would make me a very nice person. You understand that, don't you?

THOR: *No comprendo.*

GRACE: Well, I know you're being that way because you love your mother, and you don't want to hurt her, and I think that's nice of you. But I love your mother, too. We just have different ways of showing it. And I hope someday you'll understand that, and then we could be friends. Because I'd like for us to be friends.

THOR: Why, are your friends all dead?

[CARLA *reenters.*]

CARLA: Give me the goddamn keys. I'll take the car, I'll go get my *liquor,* and I'll drink myself to sleep.

GRACE: I could let you do that. I could. But it wouldn't just be *one* person that was drinking the liquor, now would it?

THOR: No, I'd have some, too.

GRACE: And I think we ought to consider *that* person as well.

CARLA: *How,* Grace? You explain it to me.

GRACE: How what?

CARLA: If that's what you believe. Let's hear your analysis.

GRACE: This is not the time.

CARLA: Lay it out for me.

GRACE: At the proper time.

CARLA: Because I'm frankly *stumped.* Because you see, I was under the impression that I would have to have taken certain *steps.* Do you follow, Grace?

GRACE: Thor?

CARLA: And if I *haven't* taken those steps, Grace, and I *haven't* taken them . . .

GRACE: Back to bed, please.

CARLA: *I haven't taken them.* Do you hear what I am saying? *I haven't.* So you explain it to me. Explain the medical mystery.

GRACE: It's not really such a mystery, is it?

CARLA: You're either calling me a *liar* or you're calling me a *whore.* I'd just like to know which one it is. A or B.

THOR: Or both.

GRACE: Thor.

CARLA: Right. A *lying whore.* So whichever you think fits best. A, B, or C. And while you're thinking that one over, you can give me my keys.

GRACE: Not in your condition.

CARLA: And by the way, let's not forget that you've got half a bottle of *my* vodka in your room. I don't *need* to go out for *liquor*.

GRACE: I poured that down the toilet.

[CARLA *laughs*.]

I do these things because I love you and I care about you.

CARLA: Wow. Thank God you don't *hate* me.

GRACE: I don't hate people. I hate certain actions. But never a person. I try to love all people.

THOR: What about Hitler?

CARLA: I am going to ask you one last time.

THOR: You love Hitler.

CARLA: *Shut the fuck up, you little asshole.*

THOR: Go ahead and hit me. See if I care.

[CARLA *grabs her stomach in pain.* GRACE *notices.*]

GRACE: No one said anything about *hitting*.

THOR [*to* CARLA]: I'm not afraid of *you*.

GRACE: We do not *hit* in this house.

THOR: So let's go outside.

GRACE: There are other ways of settling differences.

CARLA [*to* GRACE, *in pain*]: *Love*. Yeah, you're *full* of love. You're the *goddess* of love. Thank God you never felt any *love*, you'd burst into *flames*, you dried-up sack of twigs.

GRACE [*hurt*]: Well, I suppose we've finally hit bottom.

CARLA: Yeah, now that we're at the bottom, give me the keys.

THOR: Don't hit my *bottom*.

GRACE: I think, when you look back, in the future . . .

CARLA: We're not in the *future*. We're in the present. The *present*. Not the *future*. NOW GIVE ME THE FUCKING KEYS!!!

[*The doorbell rings. All freeze. Then, softly, a knock on the door. No one moves. Seconds pass. The knock is heard again.* THOR *moves.*]

GRACE: No. We do not answer the door at this hour.

[THOR *sits.* CARLA *starts to exit. We hear the door opening. All freeze.*]

PURDY [*from offstage*]: Hello?

[*No one knows what to do.*]

   Hello?

[PURDY *enters the room. He carries a paper bag and a small cardboard box.* CARLA *attempts to cover herself. Through all of the following, they remain as calm as possible.*]

   Good morning. I saw the lights on.

[*They exchange looks.*]

   I was wondering if I might interest anyone in a doughnut? I have a dozen here. Dozen doughnuts.

GRACE: I don't think so. Thank you.

PURDY: I'm sorry. I knocked. Perhaps not loudly enough.

GRACE: I suppose we didn't hear.

PURDY: I saw the lights on. So I knocked.

GRACE: Yes.

PURDY: Did you know your door was unlocked?

GRACE: No.

PURDY: Probably be a good idea to lock it. As a precaution. I also rang the doorbell. Does the doorbell not work?

GRACE: It works.

PURDY: Oh. All right.

[*Pause.*]

Actually, I'm not telling the truth. It's not quite the full dozen, since I helped myself to two of them already. However, the balance remains. Of the doughnuts, that is. The standard glazed variety.

GRACE: I'm sorry, I'm afraid you'll have to come back at a later hour.

PURDY: Oh, I'm sorry. I misunderstood.

GRACE: No need to apologize.

PURDY: The lights were on.

GRACE: Yes. Thank you for stopping.

PURDY: And I heard voices so I assumed . . . Did I wake you?

GRACE: No.

PURDY: I apologize if I did.

GRACE: You didn't.

PURDY: I didn't think so with the lights on and the voices.

GRACE: But thank you for looking in.

PURDY: I was afraid there might be some sort of problem.

[*Pause.*]

   Is there some sort of problem?

GRACE: I'm really going to have to ask you to visit us some *other* time.

PURDY: I'm terribly sorry.

GRACE: Another time.

PURDY: Yes. Sorry.

[*Pause.*]

   So what time shall we say?

GRACE: It *is* five-thirty in the morning.

PURDY: I apologize.

GRACE: No. *Don't apologize.*

PURDY: All right.

GRACE: You understand.

PURDY: I do, yes, however, I feel the implication that I have done something wrong, something inappropriate, yet as I am attempting to apologize for whatever that wrong may be, you insist that I should *not* apologize, and in so doing you put me in a rather awkward situation.

GRACE: I see. Yes. Your apology is accepted.

PURDY: All right. So another time, then?

GRACE: Good night.

PURDY: Or morning, really. Yes. Good.

[*Pause. He starts to go.*]

THOR: Can I have a doughnut?

GRACE: No.

PURDY: No, I don't think . . .

GRACE: No doughnuts now.

PURDY: No. [*To* GRACE] It's early for doughnuts . . .

GRACE [*to* PURDY]: *No. Let's not . . .*

PURDY: No. You're right.

GRACE: No. Good night.

PURDY: Better not.

GRACE: No.

PURDY: No.

GRACE: No.

PURDY: No.

GRACE: No.

PURDY: No.

CARLA [*to* PURDY]: Wait. I need you to drive me somewhere.

[*Pause.*]

GRACE: Dear.

CARLA: Will you drive me somewhere?

PURDY: Me?

CARLA: Yes.

GRACE: Dear.

PURDY: Now?

CARLA: Yes.

PURDY: Well . . .

GRACE: No . . .

CARLA: Please.

GRACE: Mr. Purdy, we have been having a discussion. A family discussion.

CARLA: As soon as possible.

GRACE: Into which you have been innocently drafted.

PURDY: Well . . .

CARLA: This *is* my house, Grace. It's *my* house.

GRACE: And with which we needn't burden you.

CARLA: And I speak to whoever I want.

PURDY: The thing is . . .

CARLA: When I am *in* my house.

GRACE: So if I may ask you once again . . .

PURDY [*to* CARLA]: The thing is, I don't have a *car*.

[*Pause.*]

CARLA: *What?*

PURDY: I don't have one.

CARLA: You don't have a *car*?

PURDY: Don't *you* have a car?

CARLA: We *have* a car.

PURDY [*to* CARLA]: Then perhaps *you* could drive.

GRACE [*quickly*]: No no no, I feel . . .

CARLA [*to* GRACE]: *He* can drive.

PURDY: Drive *your* car?

CARLA [*to* PURDY]: You can drive.

PURDY [*motioning toward* GRACE]: Or *she* could.

GRACE: I don't *drive*.

CARLA [*motioning toward* PURDY]: But *he* can.

PURDY: I *know* how to drive.

GRACE: Dear.

PURDY: Do you know the car's *transmission*?

CARLA: *Specifically?*

PURDY: I'm saying that it might not be possible. If standard transmission. Given the current situation with my *hand*.

CARLA: Oh.

PURDY: The gear shift located, as it is, to the *right* of the steering column.

CARLA: Oh.

PURDY: I'm sorry.

CARLA: Oh.

PURDY: Standard, then, is it?

THOR: Four on the floor.

PURDY: That seems inadvisable.

[*Pause. All stare at the floor.*]

[*To* CARLA] Where did you need to go?

CARLA: Nowhere.

GRACE [*gently*]: You see, we were under the impression that she wanted to go to the doughnut shop.

PURDY: I did *bring* doughnuts.

CARLA: For *milk.* I wanted milk.

PURDY: Oh, I . . . I . . . happen to have milk as well.

[*He removes a small carton of milk from the paper bag.* CARLA *is rigid, miserable.*]

GRACE: Well. That's a problem solved then, isn't it?

PURDY: Feel free to . . .

GRACE: You have your milk now, dear.

PURDY [*to* CARLA]: Have I complicated the situation?

GRACE [*genuinely*]: Would you like me to get you a glass?

CARLA: I'll get it. [*To* PURDY] Thank you.

[CARLA *takes the milk and starts toward the kitchen. After a few steps, her knees buckle and she falls facedown on the floor.* PURDY *and* GRACE *move awkwardly to help her. The following lines rapidly overlap.*]

GRACE: All right. Let's see. I think it's probably best if we get you back into bed.

PURDY: Oh, gosh. Careful there. I . . . I'm sorry. Let me see if I can . . . Maybe I should . . .

CARLA: I'm fine. I'm perfectly fine. I don't need a glass, Grace . . .

GRACE: No. [*To* PURDY] Could you give us a hand here, please?

PURDY: Yes, ma'am.

CARLA [*not entirely coherently*]: I can drink it out of the *carton*, for Christ's sake . . .

GRACE: If you could.

PURDY [*lifting* CARLA]: Here we go . . .

CARLA: People drink out of the carton, Grace, that's what they *do*.

GRACE: Have you got her?

PURDY: Yes, ma'am.

CARLA [*in the clear*]: Why does that make me a *bad person*?

GRACE: Let's go back to bed, dear.

PURDY: You're not a bad person.

CARLA [*to* PURDY]: Can you help me go somewhere?

GRACE: He will.

PURDY: I . . . don't have a car . . .

GRACE: Back to bed.

CARLA: No. Bathroom.

GRACE: All right. The bathroom, then.

[CARLA *is in* PURDY's *arms. He carries her up the hallway as* GRACE *leads the way.* THOR *is left alone. He goes to the box of doughnuts and takes one, then retires to the corner to eat.* PURDY *returns. He sits next to the telephone. He removes a small card from his breast pocket, picks up the telephone, and dials. After listening, he speaks.*]

PURDY: Nine-three-two-three Greenwillow. Yes. As soon as possible.

[*He hangs up the phone and puts the card away. He sits. Several seconds pass.* GRACE *returns.*]

GRACE: Thank you.

PURDY: You're welcome.

GRACE: I think we'll be fine now.

[PURDY *does not move.*]

    I imagine it must be chilly outside.

PURDY: A bit, yes, ma'am.

GRACE: You should have a sweater.

PURDY: Yes. It's sweater weather.

GRACE: It's *wetter* weather?

PURDY: *Sweater.*

GRACE: *I* said sweater.

PURDY: You said *sweater.* I said *sweater weather.*

GRACE: Oh, *sweater* weather.

PURDY: Yes.

GRACE: I heard *wetter* weather.

PURDY: *Sweater* weather.

GRACE: I would have offered an umbrella.

PURDY: No.

GRACE: *Sweater* weather.

PURDY: Yes.

GRACE: Sort of a tongue twister. Sweater weather sweater weather.

PURDY: Yes.

GRACE: So I think we'll be fine, now.

PURDY: Good.

[*He still does not move.*]

GRACE: You don't own a car?

PURDY: No, ma'am.

GRACE: In this day and age?

PURDY: Never owned one.

GRACE: You are an *iconoclast.*

PURDY: I came by train.

GRACE [*confused*]: But last night . . . ?

PURDY: I arrived last night.

GRACE: No, but after the train?

PURDY: I walked.

GRACE: From the *train station*?

PURDY: Yes, ma'am.

GRACE: To your home?

PURDY: I walked *here.*

GRACE: I . . . How silly this is becoming. You didn't go *home?*

PURDY: Have I upset you?

GRACE: No, it's . . . Aren't you *expected?*

PURDY: Where?

GRACE: At your *home?*

PURDY: I don't know.

[*Pause.*]

GRACE: Would you like to use the telephone?

PURDY: I've used it, thank you.

GRACE: You have?

PURDY: Yes, ma'am.

GRACE: So things are sorted out for you.

PURDY: I think they will be, yes.

[*Pause.*]

GRACE: She is a good person, you know.

PURDY: Yes.

GRACE: A *kind* person. But certain situations, I don't enjoy them, they lead to words which I cannot countenance. Things get said in the heat of a moment and then, of course, they can't be *unsaid.*

PURDY: No.

GRACE: Because of pain. Striking out with words to relieve one's pain. But of course the pain isn't lessened, it is merely redistributed. And the people today who like to talk about how they *feel* and how important their *feelings* are, well, *pain* is a feeling, too, and the self-indulgence of these people and their *feelings*, their whimsy, which they have the poor judgment to call *love*, thereby casually slandering the word "love" itself, well, these people with their *feelings* need to remember that they are sharing their *feelings* in a way that causes *pain*. Pain is a feeling, too.

PURDY: Mm-hmm.

GRACE: We all have *feelings*. To suggest otherwise, even for a moment . . . well.

PURDY: To suggest . . . ?

GRACE: That one is *superior*.

PURDY: I see.

GRACE: In quality of *feeling*.

PURDY: I see.

GRACE: Superior *feelings*.

PURDY: Yes.

GRACE: We're not so different under the skin.

PURDY: That's been said.

GRACE: We know the difference between right and wrong.

PURDY: We do?

GRACE: As long as we listen to that still, small voice.

PURDY: Mm-hmm.

GRACE: As our pastor says.

PURDY: Which voice?

GRACE: The one inside of us.

PURDY: The one that counsels some of us to love our enemies as we love ourselves?

GRACE: I believe so.

[*Pause.*]

PURDY: But isn't that the very same voice, which, with equal urgency, counsels others that the proper thing to do is to roast their enemies' bodies and then say a prayer as they begin dining on their flesh?

[*Pause.* GRACE *is confused.*]

GRACE: I . . . think such people . . . are not really listening to the voice.

PURDY: Or perhaps they're hard of hearing.

GRACE: I don't know the word "de-veering."

PURDY: *Hard of hearing.*

GRACE [*smiling*]: I suppose so.

PURDY: And don't you feel superior to *them?*

GRACE: Superior . . . *to cannibals?*

PURDY: Yes.

[*Pause.*]

GRACE: I think I'll put my clothes on.

[*She doesn't move.*]

[*Kindly*] Do you . . . need money?

PURDY: No, ma'am.

GRACE: Or food?

PURDY: I have the doughnuts.

GRACE: Money for . . . a taxicab?

PURDY: I called for a taxicab.

GRACE [*relieved*]: Oh. *Ohhhhh, I see.* I see now. Good. Then you found our missing Yellow Pages?

PURDY: No, I have a card. From the train station.

GRACE: So that's clear now. So we're *waiting*, then. For the taxicab.

PURDY: Yes, ma'am.

GRACE: I see. That's all good, then.

PURDY: Yes.

GRACE: You see, I thought how could he not know Don and Marjorie Lively? How could he not know the Livelys? That struck me as unusual but, of course, the answer is that you're not from around here.

PURDY: No.

GRACE: Yes, you see, that explains a great deal.

PURDY: It must, yes.

GRACE: And that you would make a special trip. That you would go out of your way. Well. That speaks volumes.

PURDY: It seemed like a good idea.

GRACE: Lars was blessed with good friends.

PURDY: I hope so.

GRACE: You'll be fine waiting here, then?

PURDY: Yes. Thank you.

[GRACE *studies him for a moment, then exits.* PURDY *stares into space.*]

   [*Without difficulty*] Sweater weather sweater weather sweater weather sweater weather.

[*He takes out a metal hip flask, opens it, and drinks.*]

THOR [*from the corner*]: Thought you didn't drink.

PURDY: Forgot you were there.

THOR: But you do.

PURDY: Guess I wasn't a hundred percent truthful about that.

THOR: I don't care.

[*Pause.*]

   What does "iconoclast" mean?

PURDY: Do you know what it means?

THOR: Yes.

PURDY: Then why are you asking?

THOR: To see if you know.

PURDY: I know.

THOR: Why do you keep hanging around our house?

PURDY: I'm concerned.

THOR: What's your deal?

PURDY: I don't have a deal.

[*Pause.*]

THOR: You said a buried ordnance blew your hand off.

PURDY: Yes.

THOR: Isn't that the same as a land mine?

PURDY: Right.

THOR: Wouldn't a land mine blow off your *foot*?

PURDY: I was crawling.

THOR: Some people shoot their own hands off on purpose.

PURDY: Some do.

THOR: Why do they do that?

PURDY: I suppose they've lost faith in the objectives of the campaign.

THOR: Or because they're faggoty cowards.

[*Pause.*]

Are you a fag?

PURDY: No.

THOR: Are you a communist?

PURDY: No.

THOR: I am.

PURDY: Okay.

THOR: What's so great about America?

PURDY: I didn't say it was.

THOR: You're the one fighting for it.

PURDY: Not anymore.

[*Pause.*]

I suppose it's the best of several unappealing options.

THOR: I know how to make a flamethrower.

PURDY: So you said.

[CARLA *appears from the hallway, wrapped in a blanket. She is extremely weak. She leans against a wall.*]

CARLA: I can help you shift.

[PURDY *stands.* THOR *exits to the bathroom.*]

If you can work the accelerator and the brake and the clutch, then I can work the gear shift.

PURDY: I called a taxi.

CARLA: No no no. Wait. No. Where are you going?

PURDY: Wherever you want.

CARLA: Oh. Oh. Is it here?

PURDY: Not yet. Soon.

CARLA: Oh. Thank you. Thank you very much.

PURDY: Shh.

CARLA: Thank you.

[*Very carefully,* CARLA *makes her way to the sofa.* PURDY *tries to help.*]

PURDY: Can I get you something? Glass of water?

[CARLA *shakes her head.*]

    Or a Coca-Cola? Some people, that settles their stomach. Or crackers. Some people put crackers in milk. Doesn't appeal to me.

[THOR *comes out of the bathroom with a can of hair spray. He passes through to the kitchen without stopping.*]

    Are you warm enough? Blanket's pretty thin. I could turn up the thermostat.

[*She does not respond.*]

    Your son says he's a communist.

[CARLA *puts her hand to her head.*]

    Do you feel warm? You might be running a fever. Do you mind if I . . . ?

[*He touches her forehead very gently.*]

    Don't seem to be. But maybe a couple of aspirin. To be on the safe side.

[*He looks at the clock.*]

    I think your clock might be slow. Not that Marx wasn't a great man. He was. In my opinion, he just doesn't go far enough. For example, the classic analogy of private property and theft. Not that it isn't *true,* but in his idealism, he misses the bigger picture, namely, that all *happiness* is theft. Because obviously there's a finite *amount* of *happiness.* It doesn't keep *growing,* in fact, it's *unhappiness* that grows, because the number of parties competing for the limited supply of *happiness* keeps on growing . . .

[CARLA *covers her face.*]

. . . exponentially. How's that pillow? You could probably use another. Back support. Would that help? Or maybe if I just stopped talking. That might be the thing.

CARLA: No.

PURDY: Oh. All right.

CARLA: Keep talking.

PURDY: Okay.

CARLA: I like that you're talking.

PURDY: All right.

[*Pause.*]

CARLA: But now you stopped.

PURDY: Sorry.

CARLA: Anything.

PURDY: Uh.

CARLA: A story.

PURDY: Feel self-conscious now.

CARLA: Or a joke.

PURDY: All right. Uh. Let me see. I heard one. One was told to me. Let me . . . Yes. All right. A man . . . No, wait. A man . . . *Yes,* the man is a *butcher,* and he's working in his *butcher shop.* And he's working, I suppose is the idea. In the shop. And while he's working, he accidentally backs into the . . . not the slicer, no, the other one, the meat grinder. He's working and he backs into the meat grinder, and the joke is that he gets a little *behind* in his work. More of a pun, really.

CARLA: Maybe a story.

PURDY: Let me think.

CARLA: Where did you grow up?

PURDY: A house like this.

CARLA: What did you like to do?

PURDY: In the house?

CARLA: As a boy.

PURDY: Think about things.

CARLA: But what did you *do?*

PURDY: I spent a lot of time in my room. Reading.

CARLA: What books?

PURDY: Encyclopedia.

CARLA: What about your family?

PURDY: What about them?

CARLA: What were they like?

PURDY: There was my mother. And my father.

CARLA: Did you have a brother?

PURDY: No.

CARLA: Maybe if you had.

PURDY: Maybe what?

CARLA: You wouldn't have spent so much time in your room.

PURDY: I liked being in my room.

CARLA: Still.

PURDY: What should I have done? Play *football*?

[*He takes out his flask and drinks. He offers it to* CARLA.]

CARLA: I don't drink anymore.

PURDY: Neither do I.

[*She takes it from him and drinks. From outside, the sound of a car approaching.* PURDY *exits quickly to the front door. The noise passes. He returns.*]

Garbage truck.

[*Beat.*]

I had a sister.

CARLA: Older?

PURDY: Younger.

CARLA: Did you like her?

PURDY: Everybody liked her. They still do.

CARLA: Where is she?

PURDY: Married. Participating in the marriage fantasy.

CARLA: Was she pretty?

PURDY: Very pretty.

CARLA: Beautiful?

PURDY: At the time. She was the first girl I ever kissed.

CARLA: As practice?

PURDY: Well, I was very quiet.

CARLA: You were shy.

PURDY: No. I could *move* quietly. I could walk into a room and leave it so that no one would know.

CARLA: Oh.

PURDY: Something I taught myself. I'd wait for my sister to go to sleep. I'd see her light go off. Then I'd wait thirty minutes and I'd walk down the hall very quietly. And I'd go into her room and kiss her. For practice, yes. For the future.

CARLA: She didn't wake up?

[*He sits again.*]

PURDY: Well, that's the funny thing. I wondered that myself. I mean, let's say you're asleep. You're fast asleep and someone comes into your room and kisses you. You'd wake up, wouldn't you? Of course you would. No matter how quiet they were. Of course you would. And in that case, she was awake all along.

CARLA: Why don't you ask her?

PURDY: She'd never admit it.

CARLA: That she was awake?

PURDY: That she wanted to be kissed.

[GRACE *enters. She is dressed.* CARLA *makes no attempt to hide the flask.*]

GRACE: So this is where we are.

PURDY: Yes, ma'am.

GRACE: I put my clothes on because it seems that no one is going back to sleep.

PURDY: That seems reasonable.

[*She watches them.*]

GRACE: We're still waiting on that taxicab, then?

PURDY: Yes, ma'am.

GRACE: And I take it that's liquor that you're drinking.

PURDY: It is.

GRACE: I assume that belongs to you.

PURDY: Yes, ma'am.

GRACE: You see, I thought that we had decided that she was going back to bed.

PURDY: I don't know. I didn't take part in that decision.

GRACE: But it seems now she's changed her mind.

PURDY: Apparently she has.

GRACE: You offer a stronger incentive.

PURDY: I can't speak to that.

GRACE: You offer the incentive that she wants. That's fairly clear. I have to say I'm a bit surprised. I presumed better judgment on your part. But at least now she has what she wants.

PURDY: I can't speak for her, ma'am. I can only speak for myself.

GRACE: Well, let's ask her, then. Would you like to go back to bed, dear?

CARLA: No thanks.

GRACE: There we are. You're content to sit here, then. Your needs have been met.

CARLA: I'm not going to sit here.

GRACE: You're not.

CARLA: I already told you that.

GRACE: I see. [*To* PURDY] So it wasn't necessarily for *yourself* that you called the taxicab, is that right?

PURDY: Not necessarily.

[*Pause.*]

GRACE: Well, I suppose that's another lesson for me, then. A lesson about my own irrelevance and obsolescence.

PURDY: Do you mean because your beauty has faded?

GRACE: No. That's not what I mean. I didn't mean that at all. I mean because you seem to have everything she needs. You bring milk and you bring liquor and you bring the means to her freedom. So any further contribution from me seems irrelevant, doesn't it?

PURDY: I don't know.

GRACE: Why, certainly it does.

[*Pause.*]

And where will the two of you go? In your *taxicab*?

PURDY: I believe that's up to her, really.

CARLA: Well, obviously somewhere where we can *fuck*, Grace, a warm place to *fuck*, because you know me, I can't ever get *fucked* enough, so we'll find a barn somewhere and he'll bend me over in the hay and *fuck* me like there's no tomorrow.

[GRACE *takes the keys from her pocket and places them on the table.*]

GRACE: All right, then. Here are your car keys, dear. I don't want it to be said that I interfered with your plans to hurt yourself once again. You do as you wish.

CARLA [*to herself*]: *Hurt* myself?

[GRACE *starts to go, then stops.*]

GRACE [*to* PURDY]: But I think if that is what you believe, Mr. Purdy, if *that* is your notion of *beauty*, then I must say I think that notion is very *immature*. Extremely so.

CARLA [*to* GRACE]: I wasn't trying to *hurt* myself.

GRACE: And that's all I will say.

[GRACE *exits.* CARLA *calls after her.*]

CARLA: Why would I need to *hurt* myself? Huh? Hasn't that already been *accomplished*? [*To* PURDY] I mean, okay, if I spend my Fourth of July prancing around in a . . . oh Jesus, in a *bikini* and *high heels* trying to screw a couple of frat boys who only want to finish their last free beer and get the hell out of here . . . I mean . . . And then to wake up the next morning on the floor with a bottle because you needed to forget what an idiot you made of yourself, to wake up to the news that your *husband* . . . I mean, somewhere between the time that I'm standing next to my *dead husband* who is now on *exhibit,* between *that* and the point where I'm tied down hands and feet, in a *hospital,* knocked out on *Thorazine* for nine, ten hours at a stretch, just to be extra sure I don't *hurt myself* . . . *Somewhere* in there, couldn't someone, at *some point,* just have walked over and said holy *shit,* lady. Wow, Carla, I gotta tell ya, all things considered, you must feel . . . really . . . *really* . . . [*barely bringing herself to say the word*] sad.

[*Pause.* PURDY *moves closer to her.*]

PURDY: May I . . . I know that this may not be the most . . . the optimal moment for such a . . . There's something I'd . . . I wonder if I could speak to you . . . from my heart?

[*He sits. As he does so, we hear an audible fart. Their eyes meet.* CARLA *laughs hard.*]

CARLA: Did you *fart?*

PURDY [*gravely*]: That wasn't me.

[*She laughs harder.*]

    It wasn't.

CARLA: You *farted.*

PURDY: I didn't.

CARLA: Must be those *doughnuts.*

PURDY: No, I . . . It wasn't . . .

CARLA: You need some milk of magnesia.

PURDY: Really.

CARLA: He who *smelt* it . . .

PURDY: Really, though. I didn't.

[*She points to the sofa.*]

CARLA: It's Thor's.

[PURDY *pulls a whoopee cushion from under his seat.*]

His father sends him things. Once a month. You're sitting in Grace's spot. Thor has her convinced that she has a little *problem.*

PURDY: I can see the humor in that.

CARLA: *Sent,* I should say. *Used to send.* From a novelty company. We don't know what happened to the last package.

PURDY: So *Lars* used to send the jokes and novelties.

CARLA: Or did you actually fart?

PURDY: No. Really. I . . . was attempting to say . . .

CARLA: That you *farted?*

PURDY: No.

[GRACE *enters. She carries a small bottle of vodka. She places it on the table next to* CARLA*'s keys.*]

GRACE: This is from your car, dear. I return it to you.

[CARLA *and* PURDY *start to smile.*]

Your taxi service seems less than reliable. I hope you are aware, dear, that Mr. Purdy, whose first name, I might add, we do not even know, that he is not a part of this community. He knows neither Don *nor* Marjorie Lively. He has never owned a *car*. These are the sort of things that I myself would want to know before I got into a taxicab with a person.

CARLA [*to* PURDY]: What's your first name?

PURDY: It's Nelson.

CARLA: Could be worse.

PURDY: I could only have one hand.

[CARLA *and* PURDY *try not to laugh.*]

That's funny. I could never play the piano *before.*

[*They bust up laughing.*]

GRACE: I'll never understand why people of intelligence and originality turn to drink. I'll never understand.

CARLA [*laughing, almost kindly*]: Oh, Grace. That's simple. We drink because of people like *you.*

[GRACE *exits to her room.* PURDY *and* CARLA *go on giggling for a few seconds. Then silence.*]

So. What did he say about me?

PURDY: Who?

CARLA [*giving him a look*]: Who do you think?

PURDY: He . . . didn't say anything.

CARLA: Come on. I want to know.

PURDY: Not to me.

CARLA [*laughing*]: You didn't call him *Whitey*, did you?

PURDY: I wanted to say . . .

CARLA: Do they still call him that?

PURDY: Let's not talk about him.

CARLA: No, come on. I want to know something he said.

PURDY: Uh . . .

CARLA: Or a story. It's stupid of me. I know. Just a story. Anything. Not about me. I don't care about *me*. Just something stupid. A joke. [*Remembering* PURDY'*s attempt*] Uh, well. Maybe not a *joke*.

PURDY [*rising*]: I need to call about that taxi.

CARLA: Something you did together. Oh oh oh. Did he tell you about *Mexico*? He had to have told you about *Mexico* . . .

PURDY: I'm just going to call to check.

CARLA: I just want to know what *happ*—

[*She tries to stand but immediately doubles over. She grabs her stomach. The pain is much worse. She grips the arm of the sofa.*]

Owww. Owwwww. Shit. Owwwwww. Jesus. Owwwwwww. Why can't I just know what happened? Owwwww. Why can't I *know what's happening?!! I DON'T KNOW WHAT'S HAPPENING TO ME* . . .

PURDY: Shhh . . .

CARLA [*in tears, baffled*]: I loved him so much.

PURDY: No, no.

CARLA: I miss him so much.

PURDY: No.

[GRACE *comes out of her room and goes into* THOR'S *room.* PURDY *hands* CARLA *some tissues. She blows her nose.*]

CARLA: Sorry.

[GRACE *passes through.*]

GRACE: Is Thor in here?

[PURDY *shakes his head.*]

He's not in his room.

[*She exits to the front door.*]

[*Calling from offstage*] Thor? Thor?

PURDY [*looking at his watch*]: Uh . . . I know . . . that it would be premature of me, at this point, to introduce this topic, I mean, it's such a historically ill-defined and ambiguous notion, pathetic, really, the concept for which more lives have arguably been lost, next to the concept of a *god*, this concept of *love*, a word best spoken through clenched teeth, however, given the urgent nature of your predicament, I suppose one is forced to fall back on a word like "love" in order to explain his feelings and to . . . I . . .

[CARLA *stares at him blankly.* PURDY *sits by her side.*]

I'm not making much sense. I'm trying to say, in a roundabout way, and I do hope you won't *laugh* at this, it's rather important to me that you don't *laugh,* and I don't think you will, because I'm fairly certain that the feeling is at least partly reciprocal, the feeling that I previously mentioned, but . . . well. Do you have any idea what I am trying to say?

[*Long pause.* CARLA *studies him.*]

CARLA: What predicament?

PURDY: What do you mean?

CARLA: You said given my predicament. What predicament?

PURDY: That wasn't really the point.

CARLA: No. What predicament are you talking about?

PURDY: Well. You're going to have a child.

[*Pause.*]

CARLA: I didn't say that.

PURDY: No.

CARLA: Did Grace tell you that?

PURDY: No.

CARLA: Did Thor?

PURDY: No.

[*Longer pause.*]

CARLA: You didn't know my husband, did you?

PURDY: As I said, I was at the hospital *myself.*

CARLA: Did you?

PURDY: I had just lost my *hand.*

CARLA: But you didn't know him.

PURDY: It was late at night. Your door was open. I looked in. I was very quiet. You spoke to me.

CARLA: About a jar full of snakes.

PURDY: You asked me to untie your hands. I said no one is going to hurt you. And I didn't want you to hurt yourself. You said go fuck yourself, I'll hate you for as long as you live.

CARLA: And you left the room. Then you left. Didn't you?

PURDY: You were so beautiful. You were the most beautiful thing I'd ever seen.

[*A car horn sounds outside.*]

CARLA: If Grace didn't tell you that. And if Thor didn't. Then why would *you* think that?

PURDY: But it's true, isn't it? Isn't it true?

[CARLA *understands. She begins laughing in disbelief.*]

Don't. Please don't laugh at me. It's true, isn't it?

[GRACE *enters. Her hearing aid is making its high-pitched whistling noise.*]

GRACE: Your taxicab is here.

CARLA [*to* PURDY]: No. *No,* as a matter of fact. It *isn't.* It isn't true.

PURDY: Don't laugh.

CARLA: I'm sorry. But *it isn't true.*

PURDY: Are you sure?

CARLA: *Oh, yes.* I'm sure.

GRACE: I don't know how long the driver intends to wait.

CARLA: I'm *absolutely* sure.

PURDY [*turning to* GRACE]: Ma'am?

GRACE: Yes?

CARLA: It's *definitely* not true.

PURDY: Your device.

[THOR *enters from the kitchen. He has the can of hair spray and a cigarette lighter.*]

THOR: Watch this. Look.

PURDY: There's a noise.

GRACE: Is what?

THOR: Look over here.

PURDY: Your device is making a whistling noise.

GRACE: Divises *what?*

THOR: Look at this.

PURDY [*pointing to her head*]: That.

GRACE: What? Where?

THOR: Hey.

PURDY: *It's making a noise.*

[*The horn honks again.*]

THOR: *Hey!*

GRACE [*to* PURDY]: I don't know what you're *pointing* at.

THOR [*bellowing*]: WATCH THIS!! PAY ATTENTION!! I HAVE A FLAMETHROWER!!!!!

[THOR *ignites the stream from the hair spray can. A burst of flame illuminates the room.*]

GRACE: THOR! NO FIRE IN THE HOUSE!! NEVER, EVER FIRE IN THE HOUSE!!!!

[PURDY *takes the can of hair spray from* THOR *and slaps him across the face.* THOR *stares back at him.* CARLA *stands. The blanket falls away. The blanket and the back of her nightgown are stained with a generous amount of blood. The others see this.* CARLA *sees it, too, and begins to laugh. The taxi horn sounds again.*]

[*Quietly*] That taxi is going to leave if no one stops it.

[PURDY *approaches* GRACE. *He reaches to her and adjusts the hearing aid. The noise stops.* PURDY *exits.*]

CARLA: I need my coat.

GRACE: I'll get it for you.

[GRACE *goes to the closet.*]

THOR [*quietly*]: I've been waiting eight and a half weeks for my package from the Johnson Smith Novelty Company. No one gives a shit if it comes or not.

GRACE [*to* CARLA]: Here you are. Give me your arm.

CARLA [*almost giddy*]: I'm *innocent,* Grace.

GRACE: There we go. Now the other.

THOR: No one pays the slightest attention.

GRACE: And let's get your slippers on.

THOR: No one cares. Money down the drain.

GRACE: Here. Let me help you.

CARLA: I'm *innocent.*

GRACE: I do wish you had told me where you wanted to go.

THOR [*calmly*]: The package or the money. I don't care. I'd rather have the money.

GRACE [*also calmly*]: What package are you talking about?

THOR: From Johnson Smith Novelty Company.

GRACE: That came three weeks ago.

THOR: It did not.

GRACE: I put it in your closet.

THOR: Why didn't you tell me?

GRACE: I did tell you.

THOR: No, you didn't.

GRACE: I thought I did.

THOR: Think harder next time.

GRACE: All right.

THOR: You're *senile.*

[THOR *exits to his room.*]

GRACE: I'll get your scarf.

[*She goes to the closet.* PURDY *returns.*]

PURDY: He's waiting.

GRACE: Thank you.

PURDY: Can I help?

GRACE: We're fine.

PURDY: I feel some responsibility.

GRACE: We'll be fine.

CARLA [*to* GRACE]: Will you come with me?

GRACE: Well, Mr. Purdy called the taxi.

CARLA: I'd prefer it.

PURDY: Either way.

GRACE: All right. I'd be happy to.

[GRACE *goes to the closet for her coat.* CARLA *takes another look at* PURDY. *Now she laughs hard.* GRACE *approaches.*]

Let's tuck your scarf in.

CARLA: What about the pastor?

GRACE: We'll call and reschedule.

CARLA [*to* GRACE]: Touch up your lipstick if you want.

GRACE: I don't need to.

[CARLA *grabs her stomach again.* GRACE *begins moving her toward the door.*]

CARLA: I'm innocent, Grace.

GRACE: I know, dear.

CARLA: I wasn't sure.

GRACE: Of course you are.

CARLA: I didn't know.

GRACE: I never said otherwise.

[*They are gone. The sun has risen. Light fills the room.* PURDY *stands in the middle of the room, unsure of his next move. We hear the taxi drive away.* THOR *reenters with his package. He and* PURDY *stare at each other for a moment.* PURDY *moves first and sits in the center of the sofa.* THOR *goes to the stereo and drops the needle on the record. He, too, sits on the sofa. He stares at* PURDY *as the music returns, as loud as before.* PURDY *stands and turns the music off, then reclaims his position on the sofa.* THOR *watches him.*]

THOR: You saw a dog eat a person?

PURDY: Mm-hmm.

THOR: Where?

PURDY: There was a village. It had been burned the week before. We were on patrol. Came to this village. Behind this hut there was a woman on the ground. A dog had its head inside her rib cage. Hungry, I guess. Heard us coming. Looked up. Scared. I took a shot at it. Missed. It ran away with something in its mouth. Something purple. Looked like a heart. But, of course, a heart doesn't often conform to the traditionally accepted shape. Actually looked more like a football. But I think it was a heart. Could have been a kidney.

[THOR *reaches over and takes the watch off* PURDY's *wrist.*]

THOR [*as he resets the time*]: There's this girl in my class, this girl Tammy McFadden. She's a whore. She has big tits and acne. My friend Ricky Purzer says she lets guys finger her in the utility room for five dollars. She goes around telling everyone that she loves me, so I'm gonna get her to go to the woods by the creek behind the Methodist church, and I'm gonna dig a punji trap. And when she follows me into the woods, she won't be looking where she's going, and she'll fall in the trap and then die.

[*He replaces* PURDY's *watch.*]

PURDY: Your mother looked so beautiful lying there. She was the most beautiful thing I'd ever seen.

[THOR *opens the box and places it between them. They both reach in. They pull out various novelties. Finally,* THOR *finds a can with the words* PEANUT BRITTLE *on it as* PURDY *pulls out a severed rubber hand.*]

THOR: Look. Have some candy. Peanut brittle.

PURDY: All right.

THOR: I'm gonna have some.

PURDY: Go ahead.

THOR: Don't mind if I do.

PURDY: Okay.

THOR: I'm gonna do it.

PURDY: Okay.

THOR: Look. Watch. Here it goes.

[THOR *unscrews the top of the can. Three toy snakes jump out.*]

That was stupid.

[*The two of them look at the snakes on the floor.*]

Once the snakes are out of the can, how do you get them back in again?

[PURDY *stares at* THOR *as the lights fade to black. No music.*]

THE INFIDEL

PRODUCTION HISTORY

The Infidel was first produced by Steppenwolf Theatre Company (artistic director, Martha Lavey) in the Studio Theatre on March 5, 2000. It was directed by Anna D. Shapiro, with set design by Mark Netherland, costume design by Janice Pytel, lighting design by Heather Gilbert, sound design by Lindsay Jones, and video design by Logan Kibens. Laura D. Glenn was the stage manager.

Alma . . . . Charin Alvarez
Moss . . . . Robert Breuler
Helen . . . . Maureen Gallagher
Garvey . . . . Mike Nussbaum
Guard/Trooper/Bartender . . . . Dale Rivera
Casper . . . . Will Zahrn

The play was subsequently produced at Philadelphia Theatre Company (producing artistic director, Sarah Garonzik) on January 25, 2001. It was directed by Anna D. Shapiro, with set design by Todd Rosenthal, costume design by Janus Stefanowicz, lighting design by Ann G. Wrightson, sound design by Eileen Tague, and video design by Daniel Kutner. Veronica Griego was the stage manager.

Moss . . . . Robert Breuler
Helen . . . . Pamela Burrell
Guard/Trooper/Bartender . . . . Al Espinoza
Casper . . . . Joe Guzmán
Alma . . . . Jessica Leccia
Garvey . . . . John Seitz

CHARACTERS

Garvey, sixties

Moss, sixties

Guard/Trooper/Bartender, thirties

Helen, fifties

Casper, forties

Alma, early thirties

STAGING

The set is a room in a federal building—clean, carpeted, institutional. There is a door and two windows on different walls, one covered with blinds and the other mirrored. In the room are tables, several chairs, a wall telephone, a watercooler, and a TV hooked up to a VCR and live video camera. From time to time, the action may seem to change location, but no change to the set should be made except as suggested. Also, there is no music except where indicated. The time is the present.

[*Afternoon. Sunlight enters through the blinds.* GARVEY, *dressed impec-cably in a dark tailored suit, sits at one end of a long table. At the other end sits* MOSS. *Documents lie on the table. A* GUARD *sits in the corner. The video camera is trained on* GARVEY's *face, which thus appears on the TV screen as well. An on-screen counter keeps track of the time.* GARVEY *wears a puzzled expression.*]

GARVEY: Did I . . . ?

MOSS: Hmm?

GARVEY: Did I just . . . ?

MOSS: Just what?

GARVEY: Did something just happen?

MOSS: What sort of thing?

GARVEY: Did I . . . I could swear. I closed my eyes for a moment. Did you notice?

MOSS: I didn't.

GARVEY: It didn't appear that I might have . . . drifted off?

MOSS: When?

GARVEY: Just now.

MOSS: As we were speaking?

GARVEY: That's what I'm asking. We've been speaking without interruption?

MOSS: Yes.

GARVEY: Then there was no . . . lapse? A pause of some sort. A caesura . . . ?

MOSS: Noticeably? No.

GARVEY: Sorry.

MOSS: No. Go on.

GARVEY: Because I've been experiencing a fair amount of disruption in my sleep cycle.

MOSS: Hmm.

GARVEY: And it occasionally leads to these . . . interludes.

MOSS: I had asked you about the medication.

GARVEY: Yes.

MOSS: You remember that.

GARVEY: Of course.

MOSS: I said how are you tolerating the medication.

GARVEY: Yes.

MOSS: You started to answer.

GARVEY: Yes.

MOSS: You stopped.

GARVEY: I did stop?

MOSS: Briefly.

GARVEY: Did my eyes close?

MOSS: I was looking down at my paper.

GARVEY: I'm fairly certain that they did.

MOSS: I looked up. And you said . . . what you said.

[GARVEY *pauses, concerned.*]

GARVEY: All right, then.

[*He motions for* MOSS *to continue.*]

Let's . . . shouldn't we?

MOSS: If you want.

GARVEY: Time, you know.

MOSS: We're fine on time.

GARVEY: You see . . . and I'll try to describe this sensation as accurately as I can, since this is by no means the first time this has happened . . . I've begun to experience a sensation from time to time as if . . . I think this is the way to say it . . . as if a *cut* has been made.

MOSS: A cut?

GARVEY: As if, say, I was sitting in a theater watching a film and for some reason there is an interruption, I fall asleep or I go out to the lobby to make a phone call and then reawaken or return to find myself . . . in medias res, as they say. In the middle of things. And I find myself struggling to catch up with the plot. But since I have gone nowhere in point of fact, I have to describe the sensation by saying that a cut has been made—an *excision*—and an absolutely seamless splice has been made so that no evidence remains of the cut.

MOSS: And yet you feel the awareness of it.

GARVEY: Exactly.

MOSS: Strange. [*Shrugging*] You got me.

GARVEY: This might be the drugs talking.

MOSS: Have you asked if . . . Could it be a side effect of the . . . [*looking at the paper*] the what is it?

GARVEY: More than likely.

MOSS: Sounds unpleasant.

GARVEY: Nagging, I would say. Unpleasant? "Transient disassociative achronia" is how they put it. Not unpleasant exactly. A recurring . . . disappointment.

MOSS: With regard to . . . ?

GARVEY: The way each day begins. You awaken. You know that you have been having some sort of dream. It may have been significant. Even profound. It contains secrets. But the fact of your awakening has erased it completely. Like a videotape.

MOSS [*shrugging*]: Fern's been keeping a "dream journal."

GARVEY: That sort of disappointment.

MOSS: She said to say hello, by the way.

GARVEY: Do the same for me.

MOSS: So this is the . . . lithium, then?

GARVEY: Twice a day.

MOSS: It'll probably take a while to . . .

GARVEY: Calibrate the dosage? Yes.

MOSS: Right.

GARVEY: Element number three. I thought of having a jersey printed up with its atomic number fore and aft.

MOSS [*unsure*]: Oh, you mean . . . I see. Heh-heh-heh. That's good.

GARVEY: Lithium carbonate, to be exact.

MOSS [*reading from his notes*]: Lithonate?

GARVEY: The brand name, yes. A mineral *salt*. Sometimes when the dispensing technician comes by, I ask for a little fresh ground pepper. No one laughs.

MOSS: I'm glad to see you haven't lost your sense of humor.

[*They pause.*]

GARVEY: Although by saying that you just killed it.

MOSS [*embarrassed*]: Yes. Heh-heh-heh. Well.

[*Another pause. A siren is heard outside. It grows very loud.* GARVEY *winces.*]

GARVEY: Good Lord.

MOSS: Yeah.

GARVEY: Bit *strident*.

MOSS: Emergency room across the street.

GARVEY: I see.

[*The siren abruptly cuts out.* GARVEY *looks over his shoulder at the TV screen.*]

Not the most flattering angle.

MOSS: You look fit.

GARVEY: It's the clothes. My mufti. Thoughtful of them, really, to drag this out of custody for me. Good job on the crease, too. Good face on a bad situation. Temporary, though. Back into a pumpkin at midnight. [*Looking back*] Does it really add ten pounds, as the saying goes?

MOSS: Are you eating enough?

GARVEY: Yes, I had dropped a few a while back.

MOSS: I would imagine.

GARVEY: But *now*? Not to partake would be criminal. Poor choice of words. I mean, the sheer variety. The fish sticks. The canned peas. The individual bags of barbecue-flavored potato chips. Oh, Les. Abundance!

MOSS: Yes. Heh-heh-heh.

GARVEY: The palate is *dazzled*.

MOSS [*from his notes*]: I understand that the subject of food led to . . . a slight . . .

GARVEY: Ah, yes! The contretemps! My malfeasance!

MOSS: You were attempting to . . . ?

GARVEY: It is a common subterfuge among the general population to carry the occasional contraband snack out of the eating area to enjoy later in the privacy of one's own chambers. To that end, I conceived the notion of leaving the area one day with a Hostess Ding Dong concealed upon my person. Do you know the product?

MOSS: Ding Dongs? Yes, I know them.

GARVEY: And in this way I would be able to indulge at my leisure.

MOSS [*notes*]: You stuck a Ding Dong down your pants.

GARVEY: The *foil wrapper*, Les. It was an inspired choice.

MOSS: Caught some hell for that one, I bet.

GARVEY: Well, that's the thing, you know. With the general population, there's a sort of grudging acceptance. But the personnel . . . well, no doubt you've experienced this at some point, Les. The inarticulate hatred of the lumpenproletariat. You so much as drop a word of more than two syllables into a conversation and the storm troopers brandish their truncheons.

MOSS: I was a farm boy.

GARVEY: I forgot.

MOSS: Long time ago.

GARVEY: Hot dogs and apple pie. So yes, these thugs, these school yard bullies with a paycheck, these salaried chimpanzees, conspicuous in overhanging brow and adipose tissue, these *scholars* happened to notice a bulge under my clothing.

MOSS [*notes*]: You were confined to your quarters for six weeks.

GARVEY: Yes. What is it that Pascal says in *Pensées*? "All human evil derives from man's being unable to sit still in a room"? By Pascal's definition, I am beyond reproach.

[*Pause.* MOSS *looks at his notes.*]

MOSS: So just the Lithonate, then.

GARVEY: Mmm.

MOSS: No other medications or . . . ?

GARVEY: No. Clean as a whistle. Well. A *lithium-filled* whistle.

MOSS: Right.

GARVEY: Yes, you know, the general population demonstrate far less contempt for me than one might suppose.

MOSS: Given your position.

GARVEY: I think my presence is a . . . comforting reminder of the . . . ecumenical nature of applied justice.

MOSS: You're just one of the condemned.

GARVEY: Not condemned, really. Defrocked. Never looked good in a frock, anyway.

MOSS: Yes. Heh-heh. *Branded.* Chuck Connors. [*Humming the tune*] Dum da da dum dum dum. Remember that show?

GARVEY: Do you know, Les, I have *missed out* on television!

MOSS: No television?

GARVEY: Not currently. I mean, in the *past.* I was, previously, you know, one of its great detractors. Never turned the thing on. But I have to tell you, Les, it is permitted in the common room for an hour each day, and though the reception is quite poor, I have—talk of a great wasteland notwithstanding—turned quite a corner in my understanding of the appeal.

MOSS: You gotta have it for sports.

GARVEY: Do you know what I have been enjoying? I missed this in its original broadcast period. I don't suppose you were ever a follower of the *Green Acres* series?

MOSS: Not really.

GARVEY: But you know of it?

MOSS: Oh, yes.

GARVEY: Reminiscent of Twain or Booth Tarkington . . . Here we have this man, this nearly *tragic* figure of Oliver Douglas, this man imprisoned, not by walls, for he could leave the community of . . . Hooterville . . . at any moment, but rather trapped by his refusal to surrender his bucolic vision, his *faith* in the land itself . . . even though he is confronted time and again with reality. Generally through the agency of Mr. Haney or, worse still, the ghoulish figure of *Eb*. But the reality with which he is confronted is a terrifying rural nightmare and not even his *wife*, the oblivious Lisa, played by Eva Gabor with a kind of—

MOSS [*interrupting, looking at his notes*]: I'm . . . Sorry. I'm noticing here that there was some disturbance.

GARVEY: About the television?

MOSS: No, no. July seven. There's mention of a disturbance.

GARVEY: A disturbance.

MOSS: I'm looking at an infirmary report.

GARVEY: Oh. Yes.

MOSS: That ring a bell?

GARVEY: Yes. Well.

MOSS: Do you want to talk about that?

GARVEY: Not really worth . . . A bit of . . . an altercation.

MOSS: But you went to the infirmary.

GARVEY: Yes, but . . . Well.

MOSS: Why don't you tell me about that.

GARVEY [*laughing*]: Well . . . almost *farcical*, actually, from a certain . . . I'll tell you, I don't know what it is about residence in our facility that—forgetting for a moment its correctional function—seems to inspire some to . . . take up the pen and embark upon these ill-advised literary careers. And one particular chap from an adjacent corridor felt compelled to share with me a sample of his blank verse, which bore the rather ungainly title of "Mother"—expletive—"Cop Kick

Me in the Head." And I made a few remarks, which, to be fair, were less than charitable . . . and so . . .

[MOSS *has begun to write.* GARVEY *takes notice and stops.*]

MOSS: So you were struck in the face.

GARVEY: Yes.

MOSS [*still writing*]: Not much fun.

GARVEY [*watching him*]: No, but that was, let's see . . . *months* ago, and . . .

MOSS: I see.

GARVEY: So . . . is that . . . That's a little black mark for me, is it?

MOSS: Hmm?

GARVEY: Strike against me, I suppose? Even though . . .

MOSS: Just making a note.

GARVEY: So I see. A little demerit.

MOSS: A what?

GARVEY: Little black *x*?

MOSS: No.

GARVEY: One for the minus column.

MOSS: I'm writing what you just told me.

GARVEY: Sorry.

MOSS: Lot to keep track of.

GARVEY: Of course. Sorry.

[GARVEY *waits while* MOSS *finishes writing.*]

MOSS [*looking up*]: And there's been no contact with Ms. Mendoza?

GARVEY [*quietly*]: No.

MOSS: Written or otherwise?

[GARVEY *shakes his head.*]

MOSS: No attempt of any kind?

[GARVEY *shakes his head again. Pause. He looks back at the TV screen.*]

GARVEY: So how am I doing?

MOSS: What do you mean?

GARVEY: What's my score?

MOSS [*smiling*]: It doesn't work like that.

GARVEY: I can't get a halftime report?

MOSS: It's complicated.

GARVEY [*with difficulty*]: I mean, we should be able to acknowledge . . . I can't pretend that there isn't an element of *mortification* in this for me.

MOSS: It's an awkward situation.

GARVEY: No doubt our colleagues snicker about this as they would over a pornographic cartoon.

MOSS: Less than you might think.

GARVEY: Oh, of course they do. I have violated the laws of good taste.

MOSS: Other laws were violated, Harvey.

GARVEY: But I've provided such a good *laugh* for people. That must count for something.

MOSS: I find that people . . . in general . . . are less cruel than it is fashionable to believe.

GARVEY: Oh, why not? Laugh it up. Rather that than the knitted brows. The concern. "What about your dignity? What about your honor, Your Honor?" [*Laughs with self-mockery.*]

MOSS [*evenly*]: I want you to know, Harvey, that regardless of the situation, I have always had and will continue to have the greatest respect for you both as a jurist and as a person.

GARVEY: Well. Thank you. Good. Appreciate that. But let's press on. Because, you know, things aren't all so bleak. The letters and calls come from time to time and, if not containing offers, per se, they do often inquire as to future plans.

MOSS: That's good to hear.

GARVEY: Yes. So, weighing options. Inquiries. Do a little writing. Observations from this side of the process. That sort of thing. Down but not out.

MOSS: Good for you.

GARVEY: So while one is always grateful for the kind word, well, frankly, tempus fugit. Let's not waste each other's time.

MOSS: You're not wasting my time.

GARVEY: You know, why don't you just give me some sense of . . .

MOSS: Of what?

GARVEY [*looking at his watch*]: Oh, come on. I mean, come on. I'm not a mind reader, Les. I mean, Jesus Christ, *come on*, all right? I'm not going to sit here and try to *read your mind*.

MOSS [*confused*]: I'm keeping an eye on the clock, if that's what's bothering . . .

GARVEY [*aware of the camera*]: Well, that didn't look good, did it? That was a mistake. Don't suppose we can rewind and edit that out? Take two?

MOSS: Try to ignore all that.

GARVEY: Bit difficult, all I'm saying.

MOSS: It's a convenience.

GARVEY: For whom?

MOSS: Well . . .

GARVEY: You know what it is? It's mastering that illusion of sincerity. That's the part I never get right.

MOSS: Just be yourself.

GARVEY: Yes. Tried that once. Look where it got me. So, not to play the vulgar clock-watcher, but seeing as how the fat has been sufficiently *chewed*, perhaps we could . . . uh . . . get to the, well, brass tacks, you know?

MOSS: I'm not trying to be . . . what's the word?

GARVEY: Uh . . . disingenuous?

MOSS: Right. I'm just . . .

GARVEY: Making a list. Checking it twice. Of course. My behavior over the past fourteen months. My apparent stability or lack thereof. I have your opening sentence for you: "Judge Garvey's belfry, previously filled to *capacity* with bats, now shows increasing signs of a vacancy."

MOSS [*smiling*]: Good one.

GARVEY: But then there's the other agenda. Isn't there? So please. Why don't we move to that? The Freudian slip or the spontaneous torrent of tears. Whatever it is that I have to this point, apparently, failed to provide.

MOSS: You want to know what I'm waiting for you to say.

GARVEY: Nicely put.

MOSS: Well. I haven't heard you say that you're sorry.

[*Pause.* GARVEY *stares at* MOSS.]

Are you sorry?

GARVEY: About . . . what?

MOSS: What you've done.

GARVEY: Am I? Sorry?

MOSS: Yes.

GARVEY: About what *I've* done?

MOSS: Yes.

GARVEY: You want to know if I'm *sorry.*

MOSS: I haven't heard you talk about that yet.

GARVEY: I mean, I'd like to think that you just asked me that out of your own personal curiosity, because if you did, that's one thing, and we can talk about that at great length, if you wish, but if you are asking me in your official capacity, then, well, forgive my truculence, Les, but I don't believe I've been asked to respond to that particular question since the last time I was called down to the principal's office.

MOSS [*smiling*]: Harvey.

GARVEY: Am I about to be *paddled*?

MOSS: You're misunderstanding.

GARVEY: I'll tell you what. I promise. One of these days when I am back on my feet and all of this is a distant memory, you and I will pool our pocket money and find some darkened waterfront saloon and, over a couple of cold beers, I will unfold to you my sorrows.

MOSS: Well, we really ought to talk about it now.

GARVEY: *Look,* if you have some sort of formal statement that I can pronounce for you, well, let's get on with it. But if it is *histrionics* that you seek, well then, I must respectfully *decline.*

[MOSS *opens a book.*]

MOSS: I'm going to read you something from code. This is article 17, subparagraph 5. Quote: "The State shall, in considering amendment to the sentence as set forth under the conditions of article 15, require the individual to demonstrate a full and contrite understanding of the impact of his actions and the resultant suffering, as evidence of a correction in patterns of thought, in verbal or written form, before such an amendment may take place. Failure to provide evidence of this understanding shall constitute grounds by which the custodian will deny the adjustment."

[GARVEY *stares blankly for a moment, then looks over his shoulder at the television. For a few moments, a different image fades in, an image of car headlights passing in the darkness. Then it fades away.* MOSS *observes* GARVEY.]

So. If that gives you some idea where I'm coming from . . .

GARVEY [*turning back*]: Well, of course, the *flaw* in this line of thinking . . .

MOSS [*overlapping*]: Mandatory sentencing guidelines.

GARVEY: . . . is that it seeks to supplant a legitimate function of the state, the administration of punishment, with a wholly new function, namely, providing *acting lessons* to felons.

MOSS: Are you saying you don't remember where that came from? Who *wrote* it, I mean?

[*Pause.* GARVEY *stares. We hear the sound of a car speeding past.*]

GARVEY: I suppose that's your way of telling me that *I* did.

MOSS: October of '92?

GARVEY: I see. Trick question. I fell for it.

MOSS: No . . .

GARVEY: You got me.

MOSS: Not at all.

GARVEY: Little trap.

MOSS: Harvey.

GARVEY: Made me look a little foolish.

MOSS: I don't . . .

GARVEY: Good for you.

MOSS: I wasn't . . .

GARVEY: There's nothing wrong with my *memory*, Les. Medication or . . . not . . .

[*Another car passes.* GARVEY *looks at the television and then back at* MOSS.]

[*With growing confusion*] Nothing wrong with my . . . [*Stops.*] I'm sorry. Did I just . . . ?

[*Without warning, the scene changes completely to near darkness. The lights of a police cruiser approach. A car radio plays fast Latin music. The television screen shows the headlights of passing cars. The* GUARD *from the corner of the room approaches* GARVEY *with a flashlight. He is now a* TROOPER.]

TROOPER: Good evening. Could I see your license and registration, please?

GARVEY [*with great anxiety*]: Good evening. Yes. Yes. Hello. Yes. How are you this evening, sir?

TROOPER: Could I see your license and registration, please?

GARVEY [*loudly over the music*]: What was that?

TROOPER: License and registration.

GARVEY: What? I can't . . . I'm sorry, could you say that again?

TROOPER: Would you mind turning down the radio, sir?

GARVEY: Hmm? The . . . ?

TROOPER: The radio?

GARVEY: Yes. Yes, by all means.

[*He does so.*]

Yes. Well, my goodness. That's much better, isn't it? Didn't realize. That was rather *loud*, I suppose. I was miles away. Sometimes when I'm driving . . .

TROOPER: License and registration, please.

GARVEY: Certainly. Let me just take a look . . . You know, sometimes when I am driving, particularly if I'm in a jolly mood, I will turn up the radio and not have the slightest awareness of . . . [*Finding them*] Oh, yes. Yes, yes. Here we are. Yes, yes, yes. Here we go . . .

Sometimes I'll miss my turnoff, just cruising along listening to the . . . especially if I'm tired. I read an article once, it said that if you are tired while driving on the highway, the best thing short of pulling over for a catnap, the thing is to lower your window to let the fresh air in and then to turn up the radio, both of which I do and, do you know, it actually seems to be of some help.

TROOPER: Do you know why I pulled you over, sir?

GARVEY: I . . . assumed that *you* did.

[*He tries to laugh. The* TROOPER *shines the flashlight into the car.* GARVEY *folds his arms.*]

[*Calmly*] Well. If you imagine that I am going to make some kind of confession to you in the middle of the expressway, sir, if you think that I am some sort of *felon* on whom you can simply descend with these gestapo tactics, then I suggest that you make your charge, sir, which will be, to your embarrassment, incorrect. The man that you are looking for goes by the name of Tompkins, and I will be happy to offer my assistance in the matter, but first I would very much appreciate the opportunity to call my wife.

TROOPER: I'll let you do that in just a minute.

GARVEY: I will not be bullied, sir. I will not be intimidated.

TROOPER: You didn't signal, sir.

[GARVEY *blinks.*]

GARVEY: Beg your pardon?

TROOPER: I was behind you at the Pulaski exit. You cut across two lanes of traffic without using your turn signal.

GARVEY: I . . . I . . . *did* I?

TROOPER: Is the information correct as it appears on your license, sir?

GARVEY: Two lanes, really? What? Oh, yes.

TROOPER: And then you did the same thing a second time about a mile later.

GARVEY [*with concern*]: I ... I ... So *four* lanes, then, really. If you add them up.

TROOPER: Have you consumed any alcohol this evening, sir?

GARVEY: No, no.

TROOPER: I'm going to ask you to step out of the car.

GARVEY: Oh. Yes. Let's see. [*Beginning to do so*] Seat belt sticks. Nuisance. Never forget to use them, though. Consequences. Those terrible photos one sees of . . . crash sites. Split second. Twisted metal and blood. Dreadful. Ah, here we go. And the people staring. Traffic slowed to a halt. The things that fascinate certain types of . . . But now with the air bags, well, thank God for those men in Detroit. Lifesavers. Heard once about something called highway hypnosis. These people drive right into the oncoming lane. Instant death.

TROOPER: Hold your arms straight out at shoulder level.

GARVEY [*doing so*]: Of course, if you're *hypnotized,* I suppose it's really not such a bad way to go, when you think about it.

TROOPER: Keeping your arms outstretched, I'd like you to touch the tip of your nose with your index fingers, one at a time.

GARVEY: But isn't that always the way? You think what if some highway maniac plows into me on the expressway? You never for a moment think the maniac is *you* . . . How am I doing?

TROOPER: Now I'd like you to touch your thumbs to the tips of each of your fingers in rapid succession, the way that I'm doing here.

GARVEY: On the other hand, you see the lights of a police car and you instantly assume they are coming for you. Isn't that odd? Funny. Oh yes. I see. Like this? Like castanets, eh? Like flamenco!

[*He strikes a flamenco pose.*]

TROOPER: Are you currently taking any prescription drugs, sir? I'm going to take a look at your eyes, here.

[*He shines the light in* GARVEY's *eyes.*]

GARVEY: Uh, no. No. My doctor, well . . . not really . . .

TROOPER: Okay, I'd like to take a look inside the vehicle for any drugs or alcoholic beverages. Do I have your permission to do that, sir?

GARVEY: What are you . . . You're looking for what?

TROOPER: Drugs or alcohol. Am I going to find either of those in the car?

GARVEY: No. No. Go right ahead.

TROOPER: While I'm doing that, I'd like you to count backward from ninety-nine by odd numbers only.

GARVEY: Uh. All right. Mathematics never my strong suit. Let's see. Ninety-nine, ninety-seven, ninety-five, ninety-three, ninety-one, eighty-nine, eighty-seven . . . There's a little latch there, for the seat.

TROOPER: Keep counting, sir.

GARVEY: Eighty-five, eighty-three, eighty-one, seventy-nine, seventy-seven . . .

TROOPER: Sir?

GARVEY: Yes?

TROOPER: Do you know that it's dangerous to carry a can of gasoline in your car?

GARVEY: Oh. Yes.

TROOPER: Should really try and avoid that.

GARVEY: Well, the thing is, I drove a diesel back in the seventies, and I suppose I just got in the habit, what with the difficulty of . . .

TROOPER: Keep counting, sir.

GARVEY: Uh, seventy-five, seventy-three, seventy-one, sixty-nine, sixty-seven, sixty-five, sixty-three . . .

TROOPER: All right, sir, if you could get back in the vehicle and leave the ignition off. I'll be right back.

[*The* TROOPER *disappears into the dark.* GARVEY *stands.*]

GARVEY: Sixty-one, fifty-nine, fifty-seven . . .

TROOPER [*from offstage*]: You can stop counting, sir.

[*Though the* TROOPER *is not visible,* GARVEY *calls out to him.*]

GARVEY: Yes. Good. I'll just be right here, then. If that's the thing . . . to do . . . Almost counting sheep there for a moment. Sheep jumping backwards over a stile. Perhaps that's a trick one should try sometime. Hello? If one was having a nightmare. [*To himself*] One might . . . re-count the same sheep that he had counted in order to fall asleep, but count them in reverse order, that is, starting with the last sheep, no doubt the black one, and counting down to one as they cross the same fence executing perfect backward pirouettes, and when you reach the first sheep, sheep number one, you suddenly . . . [*Again to the* TROOPER] Hello? I'm just waiting here, then? Yes. All I seem to be able to do. Bide my time. Wait for a reply.

[*He has become deeply distracted. He stares out into the darkness.*]

[*Lost*] *Mi preciosa. Mi flaquita.* Oh Jesus. Oh Jesus Christ.

[*He pulls himself together as he returns to the car.*]

So you get to the last sheep, the flock empties out, you count them down, and as you do, consciousness fades back in three, two, one, and suddenly you are . . .

[*The* TROOPER *has returned.*]

TROOPER: Sorry about that. Didn't recognize you, sir.

GARVEY: Oh . . . that's . . . Not to worry . . . Shall I . . . ?

TROOPER: Have a nice night, sir.

GARVEY: Oh, that's . . . it, then?

TROOPER: Take it easy.

GARVEY: Oh, and you as well . . . I didn't get your name . . . ?

TROOPER: Jim. Nice to meet you, sir.

GARVEY: Yes. Thank you for your . . . hard work.

TROOPER: Nice hat you got there in the back. What is that, a Stetson?

GARVEY: What . . . uh . . . not sure, Jim.

TROOPER: You like horses, sir?

GARVEY: Uh . . . well. Sometimes. It's a cowboy hat, Jim. Picked it up . . . somewhere. Nice, uh . . . workmanship.

TROOPER: All right. You drive safe. Gonna snow.

GARVEY: Is it?

TROOPER: Oh yeah.

GARVEY: Wasn't aware.

TROOPER: Anytime now. Big one coming in from Canada.

[*The* TROOPER *goes.*]

GARVEY [*looking up*]: Snow.

[*The lights abruptly return to their previous levels, and we are back in the room. Some time has passed.* GARVEY's *face reappears on the television.* GARVEY's *wife,* HELEN, *now sits at the table near him. The* GUARD *is adjusting the blinds.*]

MOSS [*to* GARVEY]: Is that better?

GARVEY: Is *what*?

MOSS: The light.

GARVEY: Better than what?

MOSS: You said the light was bothering you.

GARVEY: Oh. [*To the* GUARD] Yes. Better, thanks.

MOSS: Do you want to move?

GARVEY: I'm fine now.

MOSS: Good.

[MOSS *and* HELEN *exchange looks. He nods to her.*]

HELEN: That weekend I was to teach a seminar at the Marriott Hotel downtown. Thirty-five couples from around the country. We stay together at the hotel because the hours are long and it gives us more freedom to stop and start as we wish. I had invited Harvey to participate. Usually he did, but the day before he was complaining of headaches and seemed terribly withdrawn. So I asked if he would rather skip the event, and he said yes. And that was going to make my weekend more difficult, but I didn't feel inclined to press him if it didn't interest him.

MOSS: You wanted him there because . . . ?

GARVEY: She . . .

HELEN: In the seminars, I would often have Harvey participate. Some of the couples feel less reluctant in the communication workshops if they have a more experienced couple to give them a sense of how to proceed.

MOSS: I see.

HELEN: This was not long after the third edition had been published, and I was eager to work with Harvey and the couples on the new material in the book, but his state of mind was so . . . He was not in any shape for a weekend of seminars. So, given that, and . . . other complications . . . I suppose I was, in actual fact, somewhat relieved to be doing this one alone.

MOSS [*clarifying*]: You thought he wouldn't be much help?

HELEN: Well, at this time, Les, Harvey and I had not had a healthy sexual life, or any sex life, really, for about four years.

GARVEY [*quietly, to her*]: Five.

HELEN: That's not right.

GARVEY: It was.

HELEN: It depends on how you count.

GARVEY: It was five.

HELEN: When did Phillip finish school?

GARVEY: Is that where you're counting from?

HELEN: No. After.

GARVEY: Because it's before that . . .

HELEN: No, it isn't.

GARVEY: If you want to be precise.

HELEN: Let's just say four.

GARVEY: Either you want to be precise or you don't. Apparently you don't.

HELEN [*to* MOSS]: In any case, you see, given the nature of my work, Les, the fact that I had thirty-five couples coming in from around the country to hear me speak about these things, thirty-five couples paying upwards of eight hundred dollars apiece, you can understand why things had the potential to be . . . at least professionally, embarrassing. You understand? My credibility.

MOSS: Fern has a copy of the first book.

GARVEY: Do you mean *Healthy Sex, Healing Hearts*?

MOSS: I think that's it.

GARVEY: Or were you referring to *The* New *Healthy Sex, Healing Hearts*?

HELEN [*after a look at* GARVEY]: So whether Harvey was ill or just expressing his overall distaste for my work, what it was, I didn't know, but I knew that his presence might be . . . counterproductive. That's why he was at home that weekend and I was not.

MOSS: I see.

[*Pause.*]

GARVEY [*to* MOSS]: Sort of an *oxymoron*, really.

MOSS: What's that?

GARVEY: *Healthy sex life.* For sex to have life, it's got to be a *little* unhealthy. A little bit dissipated. That's how it staves off its own decay. Isn't *healthy* sex, by definition, perishable?

MOSS: Well . . .

GARVEY: Healthy sex *death.* Now *that* works.

MOSS [*to* HELEN]: So you were away for the weekend.

GARVEY: There's another one of those in one of her books. Another oxymoron. What was it? Oh yes. *Relaxation exercise.*

[HELEN *stares at her hands.*]

HELEN [*to* MOSS]: I've said to him many times that he is never so eloquent as when he is describing something he despises.

[*She takes a breath and continues.*]

Before I was pregnant with Phillip, this was long ago, we went down to Kentucky to visit Harvey's parents. They had moved to get away from the cold weather. [*To* GARVEY] Do you remember? We were in Louisville. I was finishing my dissertation. Harvey was just starting out. Almost newlyweds, really, although some of the . . . initial giddiness had begun to disappear and, as always happens, Harvey and I had begun to grow . . . not indifferent, no, that's much too . . . *accustomed.* We had customs now. Rituals. We were comfortable. We shared chores. One of us up late with work while the other slept. Happily exhausted. Though the possibility of one day feeling lonely in each other's company had, I think, occurred to us by this point. So we were in Louisville, and I was helping Harvey's mother prepare a meal. It was summer. Shelling green peas into a colander. Through the kitchen window I could see Harvey. So thin. Wiry. Thick head of dark hair. Like an old toothbrush, that's how I used to tease him. And he was running in circles, teeth bared, making a growling noise. I thought he had lost his mind. I looked at his mother. Does anyone notice this? Then from behind the azalea bush, as fast as it could run, the family dog, what breed I don't know, but arthritic and *old* . . .

GARVEY: Toby.

HELEN: I thought it was Bonnie.

GARVEY [*shaking his head*]: Toby.

HELEN: Are you sure?

GARVEY: Yes.

HELEN: Wasn't there a dog named Bonnie?

GARVEY: I don't know.

HELEN: Someone had a dog named Bonnie.

GARVEY: I don't know.

HELEN: I think it *was* Bonnie.

GARVEY: Bonnie is a *girl's* name.

HELEN: Wasn't it a girl dog?

GARVEY: No.

HELEN: I think it was.

GARVEY: Then you would be wrong.

HELEN: Where did I get the name Bonnie?

GARVEY: I don't know.

HELEN: Which is the dog that Phillip had?

GARVEY: Ruggles.

HELEN: No . . .

GARVEY: Ruggles.

HELEN: Then who was Bonnie?

GARVEY: I don't know. All I can tell you is that I only had one dog. That dog was male and his name was Toby.

HELEN [*shrugging*]: Toby. Bonnie.

GARVEY: If you use the name *Bonnie,* you are making a *mistake.*

HELEN [*after a moment*]: Anyway, the two of them were chasing each other around the azalea bush, stopping and growling and doubling back, and finally Harvey caught up with the dog or the dog caught up with Harvey, and the two of them rolled in the grass wrestling and barking, and as I stood there at the window, it almost seemed at that moment as if I might have married the happiest man alive.

[*Pause.*]

GARVEY: I have a wastebasket here, Les, should you feel the need to throw up.

[*The siren of another ambulance racing past causes all to wince.*]

HELEN: Oh my goodness.

GARVEY: Yes. Pleasant.

HELEN: Awful.

MOSS: Yes. Little problem.

HELEN: Gone now.

MOSS: Emergency room, I was told.

HELEN: Oh.

MOSS: Across the way.

HELEN: I see.

[*A moment, then* HELEN *goes on.*]

> [*Inspired by this idea, not sad*] You know, there's a photograph of the two of us on our piano at home. We're sitting in his dormitory room. I was looking at it thinking do any of those old molecules still exist, or have we been completely replaced?

MOSS: Isn't that a theory?

HELEN: That the body . . .

MOSS: Yes. Every seven years.

HELEN: Yes.

MOSS: Gets replaced.

HELEN: Yes.

MOSS: Like trading in your car.

HELEN: Just when I was getting used to this one.

MOSS: Hopefully for a better model.

HELEN: Have I been seven different people, then? Almost eight.

MOSS: A shock looking in the mirror sometimes.

HELEN: I *feel* like the same person. I feel intact.

MOSS: That which does not kill us.

HELEN: Does it? *Women* grow stronger. No question.

MOSS: Not men?

HELEN: I feel such sympathy for men.

MOSS: Why is that?

HELEN: I don't know. I suppose I think of those species, the ones where the male performs his . . . procreative function and then dies immediately afterward.

MOSS: Yeah. Hard to see the bright side in that.

HELEN [*smiling*]: Yes.

MOSS: Save money on the honeymoon.

HELEN: Yes. No, for *men*, life goes on. At least until the day when, after withstanding so very many assaults, like an ancient city, the walls crumble and the city finally surrenders to the infidel.

MOSS [*confused*]: Uh-huh.

[GARVEY *picks at the lint on his jacket.*]

HELEN: But I say all of this because I believe, having been part of his life now for almost thirty years, that where he belongs is at home under supervision, and while I acknowledge that laws were violated, I think the real tragedy of this situation is the failure of several parties to recognize that he is ill.

GARVEY: Isn't it interesting how we, that is, how you and I, Les, the *patriarchy*, how we've arrived at a juncture in history where the ascendant party, this *gynocracy*, has come to define our very natures, our masculinity, as *pathology*.

MOSS: I think we should allow Helen to . . .

GARVEY: I found out recently that in the *DSM-IV*, one of the diagnostic criteria of my particular disorder is that "the patient shows an excessive interest in *pleasurable activities*." Now what sort of *coven* do you suppose came up with that load of fertilizer?

MOSS [*ignoring* GARVEY, *to* HELEN]: Do you suppose . . . I mean, you're the one with the degree in this area, not me . . . but are there any objective standards by which one could identify not mental illness, but mental *health*?

HELEN: General equilibrium. Peace of mind. Companionability. An aversion to emotional extremes. An acceptance of the tedium of daily life.

GARVEY: She thinks I'm being childish.

HELEN: You would want to be on the lookout for repetitive or obsessive thought. Restlessness. Sexual possessiveness. Overwhelming ambition.

GARVEY: That's what the tone of voice means. That I'm acting childish.

HELEN: Not *maleness*, per se, but it is worth noting that a slight increase in estrogen levels in men often increases emotional stability. It's why geldings are more easily domesticated. [*Laughs.*] I'm not endorsing the literal *gelding* of men, but I do think that we need to reinforce behaviors in our men that strengthen the home and the family and to discourage ones that lead to destructiveness.

GARVEY: I smell another best seller.

HELEN: I think you would agree with me, Les, that there are men, a *majority* of men, for whom family, home, and security represent not failure, not capitulation but, in fact, the ultimate success.

MOSS: I don't have any figures . . .

HELEN: You and Fern are a perfect example.

MOSS [*thinking*]: I . . . uh . . . To some extent.

HELEN: The *majority* of men.

GARVEY: And if, at their deaths, you were to perform autopsies upon these men, I predict that inside each of them, nestled in their viscera, you would find a hard, black pebble of resentment and regret.

[*They pause, uncomfortably.*]

HELEN: He belongs at home.

MOSS: I'm taking that opinion into consideration.

HELEN: He was struck in the face. Did he tell you that?

MOSS: We discussed that.

HELEN: Twice. It required stitches.

GARVEY: Two stitches. I had it coming. I gave the man a bad review.

HELEN: He isn't sleeping.

MOSS: The medication.

HELEN: It's a chronic problem.

GARVEY: A friend once said Harvey do you know what we could accomplish if we didn't have to waste a third of our lives asleep? That thought gave me insomnia for six months.

HELEN: The medication exacerbates it.

GARVEY: I'd like to point out that these species that we mentioned just now, the ones in which the male dies shortly after . . . *coition* . . . is accomplished, the reason he *dies*, for better or worse, the male doesn't simply wither and die, he is, in fact, *dispatched* by his mate, often at the very moment that his seed is squeezed out of him. Again, not perhaps the worst way to go, but there it is.

HELEN [*to* GARVEY]: Some of these comments actually might not be helping.

GARVEY: Crossed the line, didn't I? Too jocular. Right. I don't know if you know this, Les, but levity is, in fact, a *red flag*. Primitive vestigial mechanism. So, please, grim faces all around.

[*Silence.*]

HELEN [*to* MOSS]: Every . . . amorous encounter follows a more or less predictable path. It is born and it dies. And at its death, its protagonist, the lover himself, seeks to retell the story, just as a dreamer awakens and attempts to tell the story of his dream. But the attempt is in vain, because the lover, like the dreamer in the middle of a dream, believes himself to be completely awake. And the end of the love affair, tragically, like the alarm clock that ends the dream, places the encounter forever beyond the lover's narrative reach, leaving him at best to ponder its mysteriousness or, at worst, dismissing it, just like the skeptical dreamer who credits life's greatest mysteries to the spicy food he ate shortly before bedtime.

[*Brief pause.*]

GARVEY: A short quiz will follow.

[MOSS *looks at his notes.*]

MOSS: Okay, then. Right. Uh . . . anything else?

GARVEY: I'm reminded of a phrase.

HELEN: Oh, yes, so . . . that weekend . . .

GARVEY: The . . . *Geneva experiment*? No, that's not it.

MOSS [*to* HELEN]: That weekend . . .

HELEN: I was on my way to the seminar. I had gotten to the end of the block when I realized that I had Harvey's house keys with me. Some mix-up. So I pulled back in the garage and went inside. I didn't see Harvey, but I heard a noise from the bedroom. I opened the bedroom door, and Harvey was sitting in front of the television in his underwear watching a children's program in Spanish. Two dancing bananas were singing a song . . .

GARVEY: Carrots.

HELEN: What?

GARVEY: They were not bananas. They were *carrots*.

HELEN: They were bananas.

GARVEY: That is not correct.

HELEN: *Carrots?*

GARVEY: That is correct.

HELEN: No. I saw them, Harvey.

GARVEY: *I* was the one watching the program.

HELEN: I saw it, too.

GARVEY: You were across the room.

HELEN: They were yellow.

GARVEY: You can't go by the colors on that set.

HELEN: Oh, wait . . . I think . . .

GARVEY: That's right.

HELEN: There was green on the top of the . . .

GARVEY: The light is dawning.

HELEN: Like green leaves, or . . .

GARVEY: Hallelujah.

HELEN: You may be right.

GARVEY: There you have it.

HELEN: Yes. All right, then. There were two dancing carrots on the TV, holding hands. Singing something in Spanish. And Harvey was in his underwear. And he couldn't stop crying.

[*Pause.* GARVEY *snaps his fingers. The lights change, and the television screen shifts to programming from a Hispanic station. Music plays underneath.*]

GARVEY: Now I've got it. The *Stockholm syndrome.* I believe I've got that right, haven't I? The phrase. Patricia Hearst and so forth? Isn't that it? One comes to identify with his captors? I realize that this is a bit of a logical stretch I'm making.

[*As* GARVEY *is speaking, the* GUARD *dons an apron and steps forward. He is now a* BARTENDER. GARVEY *removes several prescription medicine bottles from his pockets and counts out pills as he speaks.*]

But we do enter into these contracts, these legal documents of fidelity, of our own *free will.* We sign on the dotted line. With a flourish. Without regard for the terms. The fine print. And then thirty years go by and this woman has lain beside you, there she is, night after night, the hair goes gray, the flesh withers, the muscles go slack, she is becoming one with the bed, one continuous undifferentiated mass of beige on beige. You lay awake. Hard. You could wake her up, of course, you could roll her over and try to satisfy yourself, but she doesn't seem to enjoy it very much. Never seemed to approve of the way that you do this with your fingertips or that with your tongue. Always the same impatient sighs. I mean, that's *it*, really, isn't it? No one really wants to make love to a *strong* woman. One who's going to have all sorts of helpful suggestions, you know, when you are in the . . . when you are *attending to the task* . . . one only wants a little bit of quiet *gratitude.* I'll take another of these, by the way . . .

[*He swallows the pills and holds up his glass to the* BARTENDER.]

Not a *geisha*, exactly, not a dead fish but, by God, a *little* fear, a little *awe*, is that too much to ask? A little sense of *majesty.* Why not? Can you really expect to get that from someone who has watched your own simultaneous, slow-motion disintegration into the same heap of bed linen? Sheets and pillowcases and me in there somewhere. Can you get *that* from this . . . this . . . this *grand-mother*? This wise, serene . . . I mean, it's tantamount to *incest*. What could be more *incestuous* than two people who have lain side by side for that length of time actually rolling around on top of one another and . . . [*Groans.*] It's like something out of a Victorian *madhouse*. Frightening.

BARTENDER [*handing him the refill*]: Here you go.

GARVEY: Ah, yes. *Sí*. Thanks much. *Muchas gracias.*

BARTENDER: *Hablas español?*

GARVEY: Um . . . trying. Getting there. Slowly. A little. *Un . . . pequeño?*

BARTENDER: *Un poquito?*

GARVEY: That's it. *Sí*. Yes, I'm in the process of learning. *Soy* . . . uh . . . *estudiante?*

BARTENDER: *Ahh, sí. Eso es mucha medicina. No debas tomar tanto.*

GARVEY: Right. Yes. I see. Not getting much of that.

BARTENDER: *Son muchas píldoras.*

GARVEY: All right. Still a bit of trouble.

BARTENDER: *Muchas.*

GARVEY: Yes. With you so far.

BARTENDER: *Píldoras.*

GARVEY: No . . . here's where I'm getting tripped up.

BARTENDER [*pointing to the pills*]: *Esas.*

GARVEY: Ah. Yes. *Sí.* Of course. My pills. *Medicinas.* Oh, yes. Yes, let's face it. Let's be honest. I am a veritable *pharmacy.* I should sell prophylactics as a sideline. That's the amazing thing about the position, you see. No one dares impugn your *judgment.* You say to one I'm having trouble sleeping, and he gives you this, and you say to another, I can't seem to stay awake, and he gives you this one, and you really get to be quite an amateur *chef,* really, it's just a *recipe,* a dash of this and a pinch of that . . . [*Sipping*] You know, you really do make a splendid beverage. These are really awfully tasty. My compliments.

BARTENDER: *Sí, amigo. De nada.*

GARVEY: But what was the point I was trying to make? I was closing in on a point, and now it escapes me. Always the way. The thing is . . . women, we were saying . . . *sobre las damas.* You know, Helen and I would be in Paris. Helen has family and, you know, we're all so sophisticated, so *effete,* with our Beaujolais and snails and, you know, so assured, so certain of ourselves, so *dead* from the neck down. One cousin . . . one . . . self-important lesbian *philosophe,* some writer with the gray crew cut and the brown cigarettes, chain-smoking French windbag with a mouth full of cheese, and there we are discussing someone's view of *feminism,* and we all nod our heads politely as this squat little lesbian frog, or this *toad* rather, holds forth on the evils of our gender, yours and mine, actually using the word "pig," *le vrai cochon.* And I look at Helen and this roomful of French . . . turds, and this, my friend, is the Stockholm syndrome in *action,* hook up the electrodes and study me because *here it is.* I *nod in agreement* with each slander to our sex. Brainwashed. Jonestown. Perhaps I'm hypnotized by the rhythmic nodding of all of our heads, you know, but I have become an *apostle.* I proclaimed myself a feminist. This is what I genuinely thought. And recently I'm looking at Helen's form snoring next to me in our bed, erasing the distinction between flesh and flannel, and I sit up erect, midnight, Dracula in his coffin, and I say to myself *feminist*? Good God, I'm not a *feminist*. I'm a *misogynist*! I can't tell you the *relief*! I feel twenty pounds lighter. [*Toasting*] Emancipation!

BARTENDER: *Tú has estado aquí antes. Me parece conocido.*

GARVEY: All right. Fair enough. Didn't catch it.

BARTENDER: *Tú* . . .

GARVEY: Yes.

BARTENDER: *Estado aquí* . . .

GARVEY: *Aquí,* yes . . .

BARTENDER: *Antes.*

GARVEY: Ann . . . ?

BARTENDER: Another . . .

GARVEY: Another time!

BARTENDER: *Sí.*

GARVEY: Here another time. Indeed.

BARTENDER: Yes.

GARVEY: Twice, I think. *Dos?*

BARTENDER: Yes?

GARVEY: Or three, actually. *Tres?*

BARTENDER: Oh, *sí?*

GARVEY: Let me think. Yes, I'm sure of it.

BARTENDER: *Estabas bailando.*

GARVEY: Uh . . .

[*The* BARTENDER *imitates dancing.*]

Oh, yes. Strange. That was me.

BARTENDER: *Con una vieja bien guapa.*

GARVEY: Dancing with a woman, yes. A lady friend.

BARTENDER: *Órale, carnal!*

GARVEY: Yes.

[*He looks at his watch.*]

I don't know why it's taking her so long to . . . I may have to use your telephone again. I'm starting to . . . And that wonderful tune on the . . . you have such a selection of music on that, do we still say *jukebox*, even though it uses the new technology, the disc technology? Not like the sonic *Seconal* I've collected. Is that clock correct?

BARTENDER: *Qué?*

GARVEY: *El . . .* clock? *El . . . tiempo. Es . . . verdad?*

BARTENDER: *Sí, sí.*

GARVEY: Very late. Very, very late. Can't understand where she . . .

BARTENDER: *No sé. Es posible que ella esté confundida?*

GARVEY: Hmm. But look at me. Nodding off on the expressway a short while ago, you know, becoming an absolute *vehicular menace,* but now more awake with every swallow! It's like black coffee to me. We'll make the next one a decaf!

[*He laughs and rattles his ice cubes.*]

BARTENDER [*shaking his head*]: *No creo que sea buena idea.*

GARVEY [*without a clue*]: Uh-huh. Yes. Yes. Hmm. But don't you see my point? We're *captives*, you see? And it's *voluntary* captivity. We enlist. Because that magnetic teat is so attractive, you know, so impossible to resist that eventually it serves us better to simply hurl ourselves at the teat, pucker our lips, and suck with all our might.

[*He digs in his pockets.*]

Do you want to . . . should I . . . that is, I want to . . . perhaps I shouldn't drag you into this, but . . . have a look at that.

[*He hands the* BARTENDER *a small ring box. The* BARTENDER *opens it.*]

BARTENDER: *Ahhh, sí* . . .

GARVEY: Lovely, isn't it? And surprisingly affordable. Has the bottom dropped out of the market? I wasn't aware. So, yes. Tonight is the night. If only she would hurry.

BARTENDER: *Crees que te dé el sí?*

GARVEY: Uh . . . right. Let's see. *Creer* is the verb.

BARTENDER: *Por eso?*

GARVEY: Esso?

BARTENDER: She will say yes.

GARVEY: Yes, I . . . well, I suppose one can never say with certainty . . . [*Referring to the ring*] You don't think it could be a little too . . . Afraid my tastes may be a little . . .

[*The telephone rings. The* BARTENDER *picks it up and begins a conversation in Spanish.* GARVEY *continues speaking.*]

Gracious. Look at me. The syndrome in full flower. Well. Little to be done. Say uncle. I go down upon one knee in the traditional gesture of surrender and beg for captivity. She lets me in. Holds me in the palm of her hand. Living forever at the humid anatomical axis where her sex resides. Her filigree of flesh. Mauve orchid in the crook of a fig tree. Her sex. The teat. Now entering Stockholm. Population one.

[*He holds up his glass.*]

I'll have that refill now. Just one more and that's it.

[*The* BARTENDER *hangs up the phone.*]

BARTENDER: You are Mr. Garvey?

GARVEY: Yes?

BARTENDER: She wait for you outside.

GARVEY: Who?

BARTENDER: The lady. She say come outside.

GARVEY: You were speaking to . . . ?

BARTENDER: Yes.

GARVEY: On the telephone?

BARTENDER: Yes.

GARVEY: Just now? Here on the phone?

BARTENDER: Yes.

GARVEY: Calling from . . . from here on the premises?

BARTENDER: Uh . . . *no compren—*

GARVEY: From outside?

BARTENDER: *Sí.* Outside.

GARVEY: On the street?

BARTENDER: I don't know.

GARVEY: I'm confused.

BARTENDER: I don't know.

GARVEY: Did she leave a number?

BARTENDER: This lady, she say come outside.

GARVEY: Why doesn't she come inside?

BARTENDER: I don't know.

GARVEY: It's going to snow.

BARTENDER: I don't know.

GARVEY: And the time. It's quite late.

BARTENDER: I don't know.

GARVEY: How did she get here? Did she . . . ?

BARTENDER: I don't know.

GARVEY: But why would she—

HELEN [*interrupting*]: Harvey?

GARVEY: What?

[*The lights come back up. The television goes blank. Sitting at the table, in addition to those previously present, are* CASPER, *a lawyer, and* ALMA, *a Hispanic woman.* CASPER *has a folder and a tape recorder.* HELEN *has moved away from the table. The* GUARD *offers* GARVEY *a paper cup.*]

HELEN [*quietly*]: Harvey?

GARVEY: Mmm?

MOSS: Your water.

GARVEY: Water?

HELEN: You asked for some water.

GARVEY [*to* GUARD]: Sorry. Yes. Thank you.

CASPER: People's 11 is a copy of the children's book *The Velveteen Rab-bit*, received by mail 6-16-97, inscribed "For my Velveteen Bunny, H.G." People's 12, received 8-21. An ornamental pin, silver, in the shape of a lamb. People's 13, received 8-24, black dress with white lace trim, size six, from the Laura Ashley store, accompanied by a note: "Until Saturday, H.G." People's 14, two days later, green glass turtle paperweight. People's 15, two bottles of Moët et Chandon champagne, September three, accompanying letter, third paragraph, as follows: "How overcome I am with naughty, naughty thoughts of *mi pequeña*, how I wait for you and cry, knowing that you wait for me in your bed. I will drink you in slow, soft sips, holding you in the hollow of my tongue, I caress you, my lambkin, *mi corderita*. H.G." People's 16—

MOSS: This, excuse me, this is concomitant with the period of employment?

CASPER: It is, yes.

MOSS: All right. Why don't you skip to the period after that?

CASPER: How far ahead?

MOSS: After she left that office.

CASPER: That will preclude review of a number of these items in evidence.

MOSS: I understand.

CASPER: I believe those items have relevance.

MOSS: I think relevance has been established. You can skip ahead.

CASPER: With respect, we're of the opinion that the collective weight of the items sheds light on state of mind.

MOSS: How many more items do you have?

CASPER: Prior to September sixteen? Twenty-two.

MOSS: Gifts and . . . letters?

CASPER: As well as two telephone messages.

MOSS: Let's skip ahead.

CASPER: I'm going to have to take issue with that.

MOSS: I got the gist of it.

CASPER: If I could, I'd at least like to include People's 21 and 22.

MOSS [*looking at his notes*]: I've got it all here. Are you pursuing a point substantially different from the one in the record?

CASPER: It's a point that bears repeating.

MOSS: It's been repeated. Let's move to after . . . lemme see . . . September . . . sixteenth.

[CASPER *turns some pages.*]

CASPER: September sixteenth, Ms. Mendoza ends her employment in the circuit clerk's office. She then reapplies to Accu-Temps Incorporated for help in finding a new position.

MOSS: And that was her own choice.

CASPER: She feels she had no other choice.

MOSS: That it was necessary in order to end the relationship.

CASPER: Yes.

MOSS: The physical relationship.

CASPER: Yes.

MOSS: Which had been consensual.

CASPER: Yes.

MOSS: Go ahead.

CASPER: Five days later she obtained a new position in the office of Cook, Wetzel, Pedersen, and Associates at 200 East Jackson. People's 26 is a copy of a letter received 9-24 at Ms. Mendoza's home. Paragraph 2: "Since you do not answer the phone, you put me in the embarrassing position of having to write these letters. I can't sleep. I have no appetite. I have the terrible fear that something dreadful has happened. This silence is torture. As I do not think that you mean to torture me, please respond, H.G." At this point, Ms. Mendoza informs Mr. Garvey that she has begun a sexual relationship with a third party and asks Mr. Garvey to cease communication. On 9-26, according to the testimony of Ronald Lassiter, a security officer for the Jackson building, Mr. Garvey confronted Ms. Mendoza in the lobby there and a scene ensued, which resulted in Mr. Garvey's being escorted outside.

MOSS: John?

CASPER: Yes?

MOSS: I need to move on to the pertinent stuff.

CASPER: I thought we were looking at a pattern of behavior.

MOSS: I understand that.

CASPER: Which in this context could hardly be *more* pertinent.

MOSS: This isn't the Warren Commission, John. What I need is for you to review only that which pertains . . .

CASPER [*overlapping*]: I'm trying to do that.

MOSS: . . . to the *federal* charge and which would have some impact upon the charge that we are trying to—

CASPER: That is exactly what I am doing.

MOSS: Yes. Look. I appreciate your thoroughness, and I respect your client's right to have this information taken into review, but if you are just going to *summarize* what I have right in front of me in transcript, then—

CASPER: I'm trying to make it clear that some of the information is difficult—

MOSS: There was a *plea*, for Christ's sake.

CASPER: Is difficult to fully appreciate from transcript.

MOSS: Fine.

CASPER: That's what we want to review.

MOSS: Then let's *get* to that part.

CASPER: I'm attempting to.

MOSS: Fine.

CASPER: I can't just do the Cliffs Notes version.

MOSS: You have the floor.

CASPER: This material was *coram judice* at sentencing. Any redress of that sentence deserves to be considered only in conjunction with—

MOSS: I'm doing my best, John. Trying to do a little catch-up.

CASPER: We'd appreciate at least the *appearance* of impartiality.

MOSS: Do you want to file another motion?

CASPER: Not as long as this material is getting your proper attention.

MOSS [*sighing*]: Okay.

CASPER: I'll continue, then.

MOSS: Okay.

[*He looks at his watch.*]

Holiday weekend. Traffic's going to be a bitch. Anyone need to make a phone call?

[*All shake their heads.*]

Helen? You?

HELEN: No.

MOSS: Okay, then. Let's go on.

CASPER: People's 28 is an answering machine message.

MOSS: Yeah. Excuse me. Sorry. So this goes to, uh . . . what? State of mind?

CASPER: Yes.

MOSS: Okay. Go ahead.

CASPER: This message was left on Ms. Mendoza's answering machine on the morning of 9-29.

[*He pushes a button on the tape recorder. We hear a beep, followed by an automated voice.*]

AUTOMATED VOICE: Wednesday. Three-seventeen A.M.

GARVEY'S VOICE: *I see. Fine. Fine. So is this my penalty, then? You don't pick up the phone, then? That's my little punishment? Is that it? I'm being punished because I'm a human being with feelings? I see. So, then, when we were making love in your car, did you know that you would be punishing me like this? Did I misunderstand something, because I didn't . . . Was that the bargain? I wasn't aware of that. I see. Now I get it. So when we were . . . when you were . . . So what am I supposed to do? Just . . . just . . . just . . . I suppose I'm just confused or something, so when we were fucking, then, did you already know that you were going to try to . . . that you . . . oh PICK UP THE PHONE, GODDAMMIT . . .*

[*We hear* GARVEY *breathing for a few seconds, then the line goes dead. The tape continues to roll.*]

CASPER: And another some minutes later.

[*Another beep, and the voice.*]

AUTOMATED VOICE: Wednesday. Three-twenty-six A.M.

GARVEY'S VOICE: *See, I guess I didn't understand why . . . I mean, I was wondering . . . It just hit me why you don't pick up the phone. Is he there now? Are you fucking him now? I'm sorry. Really. Sorry to interrupt. So sorry to interrupt your good time. Goddamn you to fucking miserable everlasting hell.*

[*An abrupt hang up.*]

CASPER: These calls continue for two weeks at the rate of approximately three per day, People's 30 through 54. And twelve letters are received in this period as well, People's 55 through 67. Ms. Mendoza alerts local law enforcement, who put her in touch with federal authorities. After October twelve, communication abruptly stops for three weeks. On November one, she receives the first in a series of typed letters postmarked from a remailing service in Amarillo, Texas, and bearing the name Claude Tompkins.

MOSS: This is all transcript, John.

CASPER: I'm getting to it.

MOSS: All right.

CASPER: The letter makes a request for eight thousand dollars in exchange for a guarantee that he, the fictitious Mr. Tompkins, would not carry out an unspecified threat of harm against Ms. Mendoza and, later, against her eight-year-old daughter. Acting on this, a wire was placed on Ms. Mendoza's telephone, and surveillance installed outside her apartment. People's 69 is a credit card receipt to Mr. Garvey's account for a voice scrambler, seventy-nine dollars, from a Radio Shack store near Mr. Garvey's home.

[CASPER *hits the PLAY button again.*]

People's 71 through 80 are the recorded conversations between Ms. Mendoza and the person calling himself Claude Tompkins.

[*The recording begins. Two rings, a pickup.* ALMA *speaks with a noticeable Mexican accent. When we hear the electronically scrambled, nervous voice, it is clearly* GARVEY'S.]

ALMA'S VOICE: *Hello?*

[*Sound of a man clearing his throat is heard on the tape.*]

GARVEY'S VOICE: *Where's my eight thousand dollars?*

[*Pause.*]

ALMA'S VOICE: *What?*

GARVEY'S VOICE: *I don't see my eight thousand dollars yet.*

[*Pause.*]

ALMA'S VOICE: *Who is this?*

CASPER [*speaking over the tape*]: This one is People's 74. November sixth.

GARVEY'S VOICE: *You know who this is.*

[*Pause.*]

ALMA'S VOICE: *I'm sorry you are so angry at me.*

GARVEY'S VOICE: *I don't know what the fuck you mean by that, but I'll tell you one thing, I better be getting some money pretty quick.*

ALMA'S VOICE: *I don't have that much money.*

GARVEY'S VOICE: *Then you better . . .*

ALMA'S VOICE [*overlapping*]: *I've been out of a job.*

GARVEY'S VOICE: *. . . get the . . . What?*

ALMA'S VOICE: *I was out of a job, remember?*

GARVEY'S VOICE: *I don't know anything about that. Why would I . . . ?*

ALMA'S VOICE: *Okay, yeah, so, yeah . . . I don't have money, okay?*

GARVEY'S VOICE: *Well, you better come up with eight thousand dollars.*

ALMA'S VOICE: *I don't . . . I don't . . . I . . . Why? I don't have it . . .*

GARVEY'S VOICE: *I need an operation.*

ALMA'S VOICE: *A . . . what? It is very hard to understand you.*

GARVEY'S VOICE: *I . . . I . . . I need a new kidney. And I'm not going to wait any longer.*

ALMA'S VOICE: *Okay. Wait. I don't . . . What do you want me to . . . ?*

GARVEY'S VOICE: *And don't think just because I'm in Texas, you know
. . . I may be in Texas, but I know where you are. And I know where
your little girl is, your little girl Marisol, I know where she goes to
school, and I know where she takes her piano lesson, so you better
not think that because I'm in Texas that means I can't snap my fingers and get there any time I want.*

CASPER: The call was, in fact, made from a pay phone on the corner.

ALMA'S VOICE: *So . . . what are you going to do to me?*

GARVEY'S VOICE: *What am I going to do?*

ALMA'S VOICE: *Yes.*

GARVEY'S VOICE: *You want to know what I'm going to do?*

[*At that moment, a recorded announcement interrupts.*]

RECORDED ANNOUNCEMENT: Please deposit ten cents for the next
three minutes.

GARVEY'S VOICE: *Goddamn. Shit. Motherfuck . . . You want to know
what I'm . . . ? Wait a minute.*

RECORDED ANNOUNCEMENT: Please deposit ten cents for the next
three minutes.

GARVEY'S VOICE: *Sonofabitch. Goddammit. Don't hang up.*

RECORDED ANNOUNCEMENT: Ten cents, please.

[*We hear the sound of change being added.*]

GARVEY'S VOICE: *All right, you want to know . . . Hello?*

ALMA'S VOICE: *Yes?*

GARVEY'S VOICE: *Hello?*

ALMA'S VOICE: *Yes?*

GARVEY'S VOICE: *Are you . . .*

ALMA'S VOICE: *I'm here.*

GARVEY'S VOICE: *You want to know what I'm going to do?*

ALMA'S VOICE: *I, um . . . yes.*

GARVEY'S VOICE: *I . . . You . . . Well, why don't you just find out, then? Why don't you just not give me the money, and you'll find out pretty fast what I'm going to do to you. Isn't that right?*

ALMA'S VOICE: *Okay.*

GARVEY'S VOICE: *And don't try calling the cops or your boyfriend. Or that judge. That, you know, that rich judge you were fucking, don't try calling him. You know who I'm talking about.*

ALMA'S VOICE: *I . . . I'm not going to call him.*

GARVEY'S VOICE: *All right. Don't try it.*

ALMA'S VOICE: *Okay.*

GARVEY'S VOICE: *He's not your slave.*

ALMA'S VOICE: *Okay.*

GARVEY'S VOICE: *Don't call him.*

ALMA'S VOICE: *I won't.*

GARVEY'S VOICE: *I'm not fucking around.*

ALMA'S VOICE: *Okay.*

GARVEY'S VOICE: *This isn't . . . this isn't some little game. This is not one of your little fucking games, okay?*

ALMA'S VOICE: *Okay.*

GARVEY'S VOICE: *DON'T OKAY ME! DON'T JUST KEEP SAYING OKAY! I WANT TO SEE THAT MONEY!*

ALMA'S VOICE: *Okay.*

GARVEY'S VOICE: *Lying little bitch. Are you gonna go fuck him now? Fuck him with your daughter in the next room? Is that what you do, fuck his greasy Mexican prick while your daughter listens in the next room? Have you no shame?*

ALMA'S VOICE: *I have to go now.*

GARVEY'S VOICE: *Don't hang up on me! Filthy Mexican whore. How'd you like your little girl to spend Thanksgiving with me? Maybe she'd like that. Better off with me than with her whore mother.*

ALMA'S VOICE: *I don't want to . . . I have to . . .*

GARVEY'S VOICE: *Don't think it can't be arranged.*

ALMA'S VOICE: *Listen, I think . . .*

GARVEY'S VOICE: *I shit on you. I shit in your bed. I shit in your mouth.*

ALMA'S VOICE: *I . . . Sorry. I'm really sorry. I have to go.*

RECORDED ANNOUNCEMENT: Please deposit ten cents for the next three—

[*The line goes dead.* CASPER *turns the tape recorder off.*]

CASPER [*evenly*]: People's 81 is a greeting card mailed to Ms. Mendoza's daughter. On the front, it shows the cartoon character known as Ziggy. The caption reads "Life is just a bowl of cherries," and inside, the line "But some days are the pits," below which is added, in crayon, the message "Especially the day when I carve out your cunt with an X-Acto knife."

MOSS: So, John . . . do we have . . . rather, can you give me your reading of what was being sought through this . . . series of . . . the fictive names and . . . ?

CASPER: I'm perhaps not the person here most qualified to address that.

MOSS: Yes, but . . .

CASPER: As best I understand, the purpose was to reestablish communication through any possible means.

[MOSS *takes a drink of water and thinks for a moment.*]

As best I understand.

MOSS: Right. Right. Just so we're all on the same page. Keep going.

CASPER: Almost done. People's 90 through 97 are surveillance tapes from the area around Ms. Mendoza's apartment building.

[*He picks up a remote control and points it at the television. The* GUARD *angles the screen so all can see. Grainy images appear. All of these tapes proceed in silence.* GARVEY *appears on the screen in most of these wearing a cowboy hat.*]

People's 90. November five. Mr. Garvey loiters near the front door and deposits a letter, later People's 90A.

MOSS: Um. Yes. I, uh . . . I'm not sure I follow . . . Explain the hat?

CASPER: As I understand, Mr. Garvey is attempting to indicate in a rather cursory way that he is, in fact, not himself but rather Mr. Claude Tompkins . . . supposedly from Texas.

MOSS: Okay.

[CASPER *fast-forwards.*]

CASPER: People's 91. Mr. Garvey disables the lock on the front door of the building with superglue.

[*Fast-forward to a different angle, including a car.*]

Ninety-two. Rear camera. Mr. Garvey scratches an obscene message into the paint of Ms. Mendoza's car.

[*Fast-forward.*]

Ninety-three. November eighteen. Pushing used condoms through mail slot.

[*Fast-forward.*]

Ninety-four. November twenty. Rear camera again. Urinating on the car.

[*Fast-forward.*]

And now November twenty-third. This is the night of the arrest. This angle is from the dashboard camera of a police cruiser that pulled Mr. Garvey aside on the expressway some two miles from Ms. Mendoza's apartment.

MOSS [*looking at the screen*]: Wait. Hang on. Sorry. So this is . . . ?

CASPER: It's an unrelated charge of reckless driving. No citation was issued.

MOSS: Coincidence, then?

CASPER: That's right.

MOSS: So . . . why are we . . . ?

CASPER: Officer later testified to seeing a can of gasoline inside Mr. Garvey's car.

MOSS: Got it. Wait. What . . . uh . . . what's happening there?

[GARVEY, *on-screen, is striking the flamenco pose.*]

CASPER: I'm unclear about that.

MOSS: Okay.

[*Fast-forward.*]

CASPER: This is 96. Same night. Rear camera again. The car is set on fire.

[*On-screen,* GARVEY, *wearing his cowboy hat, smashes a window on the car. He pours gasoline in the window and sets the fire. The flames grow.* GARVEY *runs. The car begins to burn.* CASPER *hits the* PLAY *button on the tape recorder.*]

This call is received some fifteen minutes later.

[*As we watch the car burn we hear a beep, followed by an automated voice.*]

AUTOMATED VOICE: Sunday. Twelve-forty-three A.M.

GARVEY'S VOICE [*not scrambled*]: *Oh. Well. Yes. I suppose I'll leave a . . . Hello there. Been a while since you heard this voice. It's me. Just wanted to see how you . . . You know, the funniest thing, you'll never guess where I'm calling from. Remember that little bar near your place, you remember, last spring, remember that little one where we, a few times, bit crazy, you know, I don't know why, trouble sleeping, so I thought . . . anyway, been such a long time, thought it might be nice to . . . catch up . . . if you could get away, even for a few moments . . . in the next hour or so . . . I thought it could be . . . so nice.*

[*The line goes dead.* CASPER *turns off the recorder.*]

MOSS [*after watching for a bit*]: Okay. Good. I think I'd like to . . .

CASPER: Just a second. One more. This is People's 97.

[*He fast-forwards. Now we see a wide shot of a sidewalk in front of a bar. Snow falls in thick, heavy flakes.*]

MOSS: Uh . . . what is this?

CASPER: Security camera outside the Ocho Ríos tavern on Fifty-third. Happened to catch the arrest in progress.

MOSS: Uh-huh.

CASPER: About forty-five minutes after the previous call.

MOSS: Right. He telephoned from this location.

CASPER: That's correct.

MOSS: And she decided to go.

CASPER: With the encouragement of authorities, yes.

MOSS: Right.

[*At a distance,* ALMA *appears on the screen. She looks about nervously. The door of the bar opens and* GARVEY *appears. After a pause, he takes a few steps toward her. He regards her for a moment, then kneels down in the snow.*]

[*Quietly*] And why is he kneeling here?

CASPER: Also unclear.

[*Suddenly many uniformed and plainclothes officers surround* GARVEY, *guns drawn. They force him to the ground. General confusion. Onlookers appear. People rush about and wave their arms.* ALMA *and* GARVEY *are led away in opposite directions.* CASPER *turns off the television.*]

Given the seriousness of the actions undertaken by Mr. Garvey and the appearance of innocence maintained throughout, and the fact that Mr. Garvey has been involved in at least two more recent incidents of a deceptive or possibly violent nature, the People see no reason why this adjustment should be considered, much less carried out. People move to end this proceeding and recommend that Mr. Garvey fulfill the remainder of his sentence.

MOSS: Okay. Thank you, John. Is that all?

CASPER: That's all.

MOSS: Okay, then. In the time we have left, I'm going to offer Mr. Garvey the opportunity to respond.

GARVEY [*pleasantly surprised*]: Oh.

MOSS: Do you want to say anything, Harvey?

GARVEY: Well.

MOSS: This is your time, after all.

GARVEY [*unprepared*]: Oh. Ah. Well. Thank you. Yes. I believe I would, yes. Let me see. Yes. In response. Yes, I have exhibited . . . eccentricities of behavior . . . though it's worth noting that a certain kind of whimsy has long been a trademark of creative jurisprudence. The notable example, of course, Solomon's offer to bisect the disputed infant in the middle of the courtroom. Would you prefer a wing or a thigh, madam? Or perhaps he was suggesting a longitudinal cut. Never thought of that. Would be fairer, really, symmetrical halves.

HELEN: Sweetheart . . .

GARVEY: No, let me . . . I have been given the floor, dear. I don't need special handling, you know. I'm not a porcelain figurine. [*To the room*] So, yes. I admit to regret. Primarily, and I hope without undue . . . hubris? I regret the impact of this episode on my ability to make a sustained contribution to the field. Oh. Yes. Just a mo—[*To* HELEN] Do you have the clipping?

HELEN: Hmm?

GARVEY: The clipping.

HELEN: Oh. Oh, yes.

[*She begins to root around in her handbag.*]

GARVEY [*to* MOSS]: Not to indulge in excessive horn blowing. But if I may, I believe this has some . . . [*To* HELEN] Do you have it?

HELEN: Oh. Wait. That's not it.

GARVEY: Did you . . . ?

HELEN: Yes, yes.

GARVEY: Could you have . . . ?

HELEN: I wrote a note to myself.

GARVEY [*to* MOSS]: If you will allow a minute.

HELEN: I wrote a reminder and put it on the refrigerator.

GARVEY: What about your pocket?

HELEN: No. I wouldn't.

GARVEY: Just check.

HELEN: I wouldn't put it there.

GARVEY: If you would, please.

HELEN: I made a special point of it.

GARVEY: All I'm asking is that you check.

HELEN: The envelope was in my hand.

GARVEY: It's sticking out of your . . . May I?

HELEN: Don't grab at me.

GARVEY: It's right there.

HELEN: You act as though I purposely . . .

GARVEY: Is that it?

HELEN: Where?

GARVEY: In your pocket.

HELEN: Oh. Yes.

GARVEY: May I have it, please?

HELEN [*handing it to him*]: Well, I don't like being grabbed at.

GARVEY: Thank you. So, yes. Here we are. This is from the *Post*. Justice Blackmun. Quoted May eleven of '92 . . . Uh . . . let's see . . . here we are. "Judge Garvey," he says, this is from a lecture series at Adelphi, "Judge Garvey is not a good justice." And here one can imagine the pause for dramatic effect. "He is in fact a great one." Again, not to blow one's trumpet. But the point being that I do have every intention of returning to the world at some point. It's not as though I intend to relocate to Patagonia and raise chinchillas, you know, so let's not turn this into a sort of groveling session. If you want some sort of climax, some moment in which great truths are spoken, well, check your ticket stubs because you have come to the wrong performance. Whereas in Greek tragedy it would arrive on cue with tears and soliloquies, this happens to be real life and, as such, does not conform to the niceties of dramatic structure . . .

MOSS: Harvey.

GARVEY: However pleasing that might be to contemporary tastes.

MOSS: Harvey. Sorry. We're short on time here.

GARVEY: Ah.

MOSS: Really need you to wrap it up.

GARVEY: Fine.

MOSS: I can give you three minutes.

GARVEY: Ah. Well. Briefly, then. I didn't interrupt the little show-and-tell session . . . Nevertheless. Mr. Casper and his client are looking for some evidence of improvement . . . in my . . . situation.

[*He reaches into a pocket and withdraws a small spiral notepad.*]

Well. It might be worth noting that I keep these little notepads with me. Make notes to myself daily. The point . . . I sense your ticking clock, Les . . . the point *being* that in the margin each day I make a small annotation as to my overall sense of well-being. Minus three being a particularly unsettling day. Plus three, an especially good one. Et cetera. Zero, average. You see. And what I wish to point out is that in the last four months, with the exception of a bad stretch around Thanksgiving last, what one sees here in the margin is an almost unbroken series of ones. And I feel . . . that is as close to an example of . . . normal . . . as one might reasonably expect.

MOSS: Is that all?

GARVEY: And whatever . . . dream . . . or nightmare . . . precipitated the actions that I undertook some sixteen months ago, I sincerely believe that I have fully awakened and the content of that dream is no longer anything I recognize.

MOSS: All right. Thank you for that. Anyone need to make a final comment? Don't want to . . . I apologize for being too restrictive about the time, but in the interest of fairness . . . Anyone?

[*Heads turn. After a few moments, the* GUARD *in the corner raises his hand.*]

Yes, sir? Sorry. I know we need to clear the room.

GUARD: Uh . . . I should mention . . . while waiting to get started today, I left this gentleman for a few minutes, unsupervised. When I returned from the men's room down the hall, I found him using that telephone on the wall in violation of procedure. I asked who he was calling, but he declined to give me an answer. Just need to mention that.

MOSS: Why did you use the phone, Harvey?

GUARD: The lines are monitored, so I can get you the number.

MOSS: Who were you trying to call?

[GARVEY *cannot respond.*]

Can you tell us?

GARVEY: I . . . I . . . you know . . . I . . . when I . . . wasn't anticipating . . .

HELEN: Harvey?

GARVEY: You know, this really is a dark age, this current . . . this . . .

HELEN: Harvey?

GARVEY: You see . . . this is . . . this contemptible . . . atmosphere of mistrust . . . and . . .

MOSS: Just say, Harvey.

[GARVEY's *mouth opens, but he cannot speak. He gestures vaguely. All watch. Then another ambulance siren approaches and quickly grows to a deafening volume.* GARVEY *covers his ears.*]

GARVEY: JESUS CHRIST ALMIGHTY!! WHAT THE FUCK IS THIS? WHAT THE FUCK IS THIS?! THE BOMBING OF DRESDEN?!!

[*The siren stops. He covers his face and begins to cry quietly. No one says anything for a few moments.* HELEN *puts her hand on* GARVEY's *shoulder.*]

[*Through tears*] I only wanted you to call. Why wouldn't you call me?

HELEN [*very quietly*]: Harvey . . .

GARVEY: Why did you stop loving me?

[*Pause. Heads turn toward* ALMA. *She opens her mouth to speak.*]

CASPER: You don't have to answer that.

[ALMA *stops. All are quiet.*]

MOSS: All right. Thank you again. I'll make my recommendation tomorrow. [*To* CASPER] You should get word by three o'clock. We're done.

[*The* GUARD *stands and turns off the television. He wheels the cart and the video camera to one side.* MOSS *starts to pack up.* CASPER *stands at the same time and packs his briefcase. When he is done, he motions to* ALMA, *who stands. The two of them exit without a glance at* GARVEY, HELEN, *or* MOSS. *The* GUARD *places the two empty chairs upside down on the table. In the middle of packing his things,* MOSS *stops.*]

[*To himself as much as anyone else*] I'll never forget a time. I was six at most. I loved my mother very much. And every night she would come upstairs and tuck my brother and me into our beds. And when she finished, she would give each of us a goodnight kiss. First she would tuck my brother in. He was younger. There was a lamp next to his bed. A small lamp in the shape of a duck playing a drum. And she would kiss my brother on the lips. A tiny smacking sound. Then to me. She would tuck me in just the same, and then she would kiss me. But on the *cheek*. Out would go the light. The door would close. My brother would drift off to sleep. And I would lie awake wondering . . . why this . . . inequity . . . existed. Did she love my brother more than me? Then one night my parents invited some friends from town to visit. We got to stay up later than usual this night, my brother and I. We read comic books in our beds. Finally my mother came up the stairs. I resolved to have the kiss I wanted. The door opened. Laughter from down below. My palms were warm and moist. She kissed my brother. Out went the light. She approached and sat on my bed. I held my breath. Sleep tight, Leslie, she said. With my small hands, I grabbed her tightly by the shoulders and pushed my lips as hard as I could against hers. I tasted what I would later come to recognize as cigarettes and beer. She pushed me quickly away and looked at me with hard eyes. She wiped at her mouth with the back of her hand. What in God's name has gotten into you? she said. She stood up and walked away. I never kissed her again.

[MOSS *rises and goes to the watercooler. The* GUARD *puts his chair on the table.*]

HELEN: Phillip has that book you wanted.

GARVEY: What book?

HELEN: You asked him to bring you a book.

GARVEY: I don't think I did.

HELEN: Well, he has a book for you.

GARVEY: You don't know what book?

HELEN: The one you asked him for.

GARVEY: Clearly, I don't remember *asking* for a book.

HELEN: Well, maybe he made a mistake.

GARVEY: It seems that one of us has made a mistake.

HELEN: Possibly. I don't know.

GARVEY: Obviously.

HELEN: All right.

GARVEY: Things either *happen* or they *don't.*

HELEN: All right.

GARVEY: It's not a great *mystery.*

HELEN: You should speak to him about this.

GARVEY: I intend to.

[*Pause. Both of them stare at the floor.*]

Bonnie was a cat.

HELEN: Who?

GARVEY: Bonnie. It was your cat. You had a cat named Bonnie.

HELEN: Oh, of course.

GARVEY: The orange one.

HELEN: Of course.

[MOSS *picks up his briefcase.* HELEN *touches* GARVEY'S *cheek. From somewhere, a beautiful old Mexican love song begins, sung by a woman.* MOSS *and* HELEN *exit. The* GUARD *stacks the chairs on top of the table and pushes the table aside. Then he approaches* GARVEY, *who stands. Handcuffs are placed around* GARVEY'S *wrists. The* GUARD *motions toward the door, and he and* GARVEY *exit, closing the door behind them. The music continues to play. For a moment, nothing happens. Then, before the lights change, snow begins to fall in the room. Lightly at first, then it increases. The room darkens. Now we are outside.* ALMA, *in a winter coat and hat, appears at the far end of the stage. The door opens. A shaft of colored light from inside the "bar" cuts through the darkness. The music now comes from behind the open door, that is, from inside the bar.* GARVEY *steps into the doorway. It is the scene we saw previously on the surveillance videotape. Upon seeing* ALMA, GARVEY *beams.*]

GARVEY: *Mi preciosa. Mi flaquita. Mi chulita.*

[*He takes a few steps toward her, stops, then goes down on his knees in the snow.*]

You see. Now I am fully awake. Awake at last.

[*He reaches in his pocket as the lights slowly fade to black.*]

ABOUT THE PLAYWRIGHT

Bruce Norris is an actor and a writer whose plays include *The Actor Retires, The Vanishing Twin, The Infidel, Purple Heart, We All Went Down to Amsterdam,* and *The Pain and the Itch.* He can be seen in the films *A Civil Action* and *The Sixth Sense.* He lives in Brooklyn, New York.

Grace (Rosemary Prinz) and Carla (Laurie Metcalf),
Purple Heart, Steppenwolf Theatre

Carla (Laurie Metcalf) and Thor (Nathan Kiley), *Purple Heart*,
Steppenwolf Theatre

Grace (Rosemary Prinz), *Purple Heart*, Steppenwolf Theatre

Carla (Laurie Metcalf), Purdy (Christopher Evan Welch),
Grace (Rosemary Prinz), and Thor (Nathan Kiley), *Purple Heart*,
Steppenwolf Theatre

Garvey (Mike Nussbaum) and Trooper (Dale Rivera), *The Infidel*,
Steppenwolf Theatre

Helen (Maureen Gallagher) and Garvey (Mike Nussbaum), *The Infidel,*
Steppenwolf Theatre

Garvey (Mike Nussbaum), *The Infidel*, Steppenwolf Theatre

Moss (Robert Breuler) and Garvey (Mike Nussbaum), *The Infidel*,
Steppenwolf Theatre